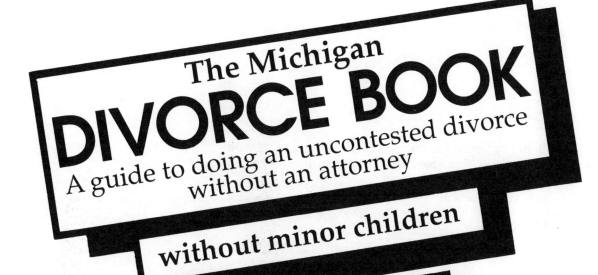

The Michigan
DIVORCE BOOK
A guide to doing an uncontested divorce without an attorney

without minor children

By Michael Maran • Michigan Attorney

GRAND RIVER PRESS

Grand River Press
P.O. Box 1342
E. Lansing, MI 48826

The Michigan Divorce Book: A Guide to Doing an Uncontested Divorce without an Attorney (without minor children) by Michael Maran

Published by:
Grand River Press
P.O. Box 1342
E. Lansing, MI 48826

Printing history:
First edition: January 1986
Second edition:
  First printing: June 1989
  Second printing: September 1990
Third edition:
  First printing: May 1993
  Second printing: October 1994
  Third printing: January 1996
Fourth edition:
  First printing: February 1998
  Second printing: November 1999
Fifth edition:
  First printing: March 2001
  Second printing: March 2002
  Third printing: July 2003
Sixth edition: January 2004

ISBN 0-936343-16-8
Printed in the United States of America

Order Form

- **The Michigan Divorce Book: A Guide to Doing an Uncontested Divorce without an Attorney (without minor children)** $24.95

    Update $1.00

- **The Michigan Divorce Book: A Guide to Doing an Uncontested Divorce without an Attorney (with minor children)** $29.95

    Update $1.50

ALSO AVAILABLE:

- **The Michigan Estate Planning Book: A Complete Do-It Yourself Guide to Planning an Estate in Michigan** $29.95

- **After the Divorce: A Do-It-Yourself Guide to Enforcing or Modifying a Divorce Judgment in Michigan** $29.95

TITLE	PRICE	QUANTITY	TOTAL

Subtotal	
Add 6% Sales Tax	
Postage	$2.50
TOTAL	

Method of Payment:

☐ Check or money order (payable to **Grand River Press**)

☐ Charge: ☐ Visa ☐ MasterCard

Account # ☐☐☐☐☐☐☐☐☐☐☐☐☐☐☐☐☐☐☐

Expiration Date _____ Signature _____

Name _____

Address _____

City _____ State _____ Zip _____

Please send form to: Grand River Press, P.O. Box 1342, East Lansing, Michigan 48826

Dedication:
V. Cramer

Illustrations:
Patric Fourshe

Lettering and layout:
Altese Graphic Design

Editing:
Mark Woodbury

Contents

Chapter 2

Doing Your Divorce

Appendices

Forms

Preface

Do your own divorce? The idea may sound crazy to many people. After all, doesn't everyone need a lawyer to get a divorce?

The fact is, you have the right to do your own divorce, just as you have the right to represent yourself in any legal matter. The right of legal self-representation is so important it's protected by the Bill of Rights in the U.S. Constitution (it falls under the First Amendment's right of petition for redress of grievances). In Michigan, legal self-help is also guaranteed by Sec. 13 of Art. 1 of the Michigan Constitution of 1963, which says: "a suitor in any court of this state has the right to prosecute or defend his suit, either *in his own proper person* or by an attorney." (Emphasis added.)

Despite these guarantees, the right to represent yourself in court doesn't mean very much if you don't know what you're doing once you get there. That's where this book comes in.

Chapter 1 describes divorce, tells you what an uncontested divorce is and helps you decide whether you can handle it yourself. Chapter 2 has instructions and sample forms to guide you through a divorce. And last but not least, blank forms are included in the back of the book which you can tear out and use to file your own divorce case.

Chapter 1

PART I: Introduction to Divorce

PART II: Uncontested Divorce

PART III: Doing an Uncontested Divorce Yourself

PART I: Introduction to Divorce

Asked about the origin of divorce, the French philosopher Voltaire said he didn't know exactly, but assumed that divorce was invented a few weeks after marriage. His reasoning? A couple married, quarreled and were ready for divorce a few weeks later.

Although it was meant as a joke, Voltaire's remark wasn't that far from the truth. Divorce *has* been around almost as long as marriage. The Babylonian Code of Hammurabi, the oldest known code of law, authorized divorce on several grounds, including a wife's barrenness, disloyalty, neglect or disease. According to the Bible, a Hebrew husband could divorce his wife for "uncleanness" by handing her a "bill of divorcement" and sending her away.

It was this law that Jesus was quizzed about by the Pharisees when they asked him: "Is it lawful for a man to divorce his wife?" The Gospel of St. Mark says Jesus condemned the practice, adding: "What therefore God hath joined together, let not man put asunder." Yet St. Matthew's account of this incident is different. It says that Jesus permitted divorce on grounds of wives' "fornication." Other New Testament scripture is also contradictory; some passages are hostile to divorce, while others seem to tolerate it.

With all this confusion, the Bible can be interpreted to either allow or disallow divorce. Catholic countries sided with the Mark Gospel and forbade divorce. But Protestant countries—with the notable exception of England—followed Matthew and allowed divorce on grounds of adultery and sometimes desertion.

When it came to law, America usually took its cue from England, so it should have observed the English ban on divorce. But divorce became firmly established in this country after the first American divorce was granted in

1639 by the Massachusetts Bay Colony to Mrs. James Luxford for her husband's bigamy.

There were several reasons for that. In a way, America itself was the child of divorce: the "divorce," in the guise of the American Revolution, from England. It's even possible to read the Declaration of Independence as the petition for that divorce. This interpretation isn't as far-fetched as it seems.

Thomas Jefferson, the author of the Declaration of Independence, had handled divorce cases as a young lawyer, and the catalog of grievances and wrongs found in the declaration echoed those from his divorce practice.

There were also practical reasons for the American love affair with divorce. During the colonial era, divorce was forbidden in England, France, Italy and several other European countries. Many immigrants to America were fleeing these repressive divorce laws as much as religious or political persecution. Once here, they were in no mood for tough European-style divorce laws.

By the mid-19th century, almost all the states had divorce laws. Typically, these laws permitted divorce on a variety of fault grounds. According to this fault system, divorce was available only when one spouse had committed marital misconduct. This gave the faultless spouse grounds for a divorce.

On the other hand, an at-fault spouse wasn't entitled to get a divorce. A peculiar divorce doctrine called recrimination prevented anyone with "unclean hands" from asking for a divorce. Recrimination effectively barred an at-fault spouse (who often wanted out of the marriage the most) from getting a divorce, unless the faultless spouse was willing to excuse the marital misconduct. By using this divorce veto, the faultless spouse could blackmail the at-fault spouse—by demanding extra property, support or other concessions—as the price for the divorce.

During this era, Michigan divorce law was typical of the fault divorce laws. The 1846 divorce law had seven fault grounds for divorce: 1) adultery 2) physical incompetence 3) imprisonment 4) desertion 5) husband's drunkenness 6) extreme cruelty 7) husband's neglect. It also had a strict recrimination doctrine.

But not every state was as generous with divorce grounds as Michigan. Before 1967, New York had a notoriously tough divorce law, which allowed divorce only on grounds of adultery. South Carolina was even worse. Divorce was legalized in that state after the Civil War and then abolished in 1878. Divorce was finally re-established in South Carolina in 1949, after an absence of 71 years!

When people were frustrated by strict divorce laws in their home states, they often fled to other states with better laws. This so-called migratory divorce was possible because the United States, unlike most countries, doesn't have a uniform national divorce law. Instead, divorce is regulated by each state. With 50 different divorce laws, it's no wonder that migratory divorce has been a problem in America since colonial times.

Many states tried to stop migratory divorce by adopting divorce residence requirements or erecting other barriers. But a handful of states encouraged divorce migration as a boost to local tourism. Nevada even managed to make migratory divorce its largest industry for a while. In 1907, William Schnitzer, a sharp New York lawyer, noticed that Nevada had a lax divorce law, with a short residence period, seven grounds for divorce and no recrimination doctrine. Schnitzer opened an office in Reno and soon divorce migrants flocked there. Other lawyers followed in Schnitzer's footsteps and migratory divorce flourished in Nevada.

As easy as migratory divorce was, it was still very expensive. There was the cost of getting the divorce, not to mention the expense of traveling to another state and living there during the residence period. As a result, migratory divorce was a luxury only the wealthy could afford.

Among those making the trek to Nevada was Nelson Rockefeller, then governor of New York. Millionaire Rockefeller got a Nevada divorce in 1962 while thousands of his fellow New Yorkers were stuck at home without a divorce remedy. Rockefeller's divorce caused a furor, and many think it cost him the Republican presidential nomination in 1964.

By the 1960s, all the controversy over migratory divorce had created the mood for change. California took the first step in 1969 when it adopted a "no-fault" divorce law. Previously, California had had a fault divorce law with several fault grounds (adultery, extreme cruelty, willful neglect, etc.). It replaced these with two no-fault grounds: incurable insanity and irreconcilable differences. What's more, the new California law banished fault from the other divorce issues of alimony, child support and property division.

The California no-fault law revolutionized divorce in America, as other states rushed to enact similar no-fault laws. Within five years, 45 states had adopted no-fault divorce. By 1986, when final holdout South Dakota gave in, every state had some type of no-fault divorce.

Michigan was among the first states to adopt no-fault divorce in the early 1970s. But in Michigan the transition from fault to no-fault divorce wasn't as smooth as it was in other states. At first, Michigan lawmakers were poised to adopt a sweeping California-style no-fault divorce law removing fault from divorce entirely. Michigan lawyers were horrified at this idea because they feared that no-fault divorce meant no-lawyer divorce. The lawyers lobbied furiously against the no-fault proposal. Ultimately, a deal was reached providing for no-fault divorce grounds, but with fault left intact for most of the other divorce issues. This no-fault divorce law took effect on Jan. 1, 1972, and is still the law today.

In the last few years, no-fault divorce has stirred up new controversy. Feminists have complained that no-fault divorce can be unfair to women. Their reasoning: no-fault destroyed the divorce leverage women once had, leading to smaller property division and support settlements for them. Some conservatives argue that no-fault divorce actually encourages divorce, bringing more of the social problems associated with divorce.

In Michigan, no-fault critics have introduced bills in the legislature to repeal parts of the no-fault law, and re-introduce fault into divorce grounds. These proposals got a lot of press, but haven't gone anywhere as legislators have shied away from re-opening the debate on no-fault divorce.

Do-It-Yourself Divorce

During the era of fault divorce, few dared to do their own divorces because they were hard to handle. But a no-fault divorce is really just a clerical task, which even a nonlawyer can manage. As soon as no-fault laws were adopted, nonlawyer entrepreneurs set up do-it-yourself divorce services to help people do their own divorces.

In Michigan, two such operations sprang up in 1972 after the no-fault divorce law went into effect: Harry Gordon Associates in Oak Park and Gordon, Graham and Cramer in Detroit. Harry Gordon Associates sold a divorce kit with forms and instructions. Gordon, Graham and Cramer offered personalized services, including preparation of papers, filing and help with court appearances.

Alarmed at this threat to their business, Michigan lawyers sought to enforce the unauthorized practice of law statute against their new rivals. Like most states, Michigan has an unauthorized practice law barring non-lawyers from practicing law. This law permits you to represent yourself, but you must be a lawyer to represent others.

In 1972, courts invoked this law and ordered Harry Gordon Associates and Gordon, Graham and Cramer out of business. Facing jail if they disobeyed, most of the firms' operators reluctantly closed. But Virginia Cramer, one of the partners in Gordon, Graham and Cramer, refused to be intimidated. She re-emerged with a new divorce service similar to her old one. Just like before, lawyers tried to stop her claiming that she was engaged in the unauthorized practice of law.

After battling in court for several years, the parties ended up before the Michigan Supreme Court in the case known as *State Bar of Michigan v. Cramer.* The issue in the case was whether Cramer had violated the unauthorized practice law by providing personalized legal services. The court decided that she had when she gave clients *specific* legal information (telling them what to do in their particular situations). On the other hand, the court said that nonlawyers like Cramer could offer *general* legal information in the form of books or legal kits.

Thanks to the apparent ban on nonlawyer divorce services, few such firms exist in Michigan. Without this option, most divorce do-it-yourselfers have had to rely on self-help divorce books or kits. Since the 1970s, several legal aid organizations and women's groups have offered do-it-yourself divorce kits. This book has its genesis in one such kit published in 1981. It was enlarged into book form in 1986, and has been revised several times since then.

PART II: Uncontested Divorce

Before you start your divorce, it's important to talk with your spouse and see if you agree on the divorce issues. This will determine whether your divorce will be contested or uncontested.

A disagreement over the divorce issues usually means a contested divorce. You are entitled to represent yourself in a contested divorce. But your spouse would probably get a lawyer, providing an edge over you during the divorce. That's why you shouldn't represent yourself in a contested case.

On the other hand, if you and your spouse agree on all the divorce issues, you have an uncontested divorce. You ought to be able to handle this kind of divorce yourself without a lawyer. But see Part III for several situations in which even an uncontested divorce may be too complicated for you to do yourself.

What sort of agreement do you need for an uncontested divorce? A formal written agreement—called a separation or settlement agreement—won't be necessary. Michigan doesn't require these in uncontested cases, as some states do. Instead, an informal agreement or understanding should be enough.

Sometimes you may not need an agreement at all. Needless to say, it's impossible to discuss divorce with a spouse who has disappeared. In that case, the spouse's absence should permit you to go ahead and get an uncontested divorce just as if s/he were agreeing to it.

Divorce Issues

During your talk, you and your spouse may quickly agree that your marriage must end. But a divorce is more than simply ending a marriage. In a divorce with minor children, there are a lot of divorce issues dealing with the children. Even in divorces without minor children, there are three important divorce issues:

- end of marriage
- property division
- alimony

These are the issues you and your spouse must agree on to have an uncontested divorce. To help you reach agreement, the rest of this chapter examines these issues in detail.

End of Marriage

Above all else, a divorce means ending your marriage. To accomplish that, you need specific grounds (reasons). As explained in Part I, Michigan once had fault grounds, such as adultery, desertion, extreme cruelty, etc., for divorce. But in 1972, Michigan adopted these no-fault grounds for divorce:

There has been a breakdown of the marriage relationship to the extent that the objects of matrimony have been destroyed and there remains no reasonable likelihood that the marriage can be preserved.

If you look at these grounds closely, you see that three things must exist to get a divorce: 1) a marital breakdown ("breakdown of the marriage relationship") 2) that is serious ("to the extent that the objects of matrimony have been destroyed") 3) and permanent ("there remains no reasonable likelihood that the marriage can be preserved").

At first, when the no-fault law was new, courts had trouble applying the no-fault grounds. Judges continued to probe into the reasons for marital breakdowns, as they had under the old fault law. Some judges even denied divorces when they felt that a marriage hadn't really broken down or could be saved.

By the late 1970s, courts were applying the no-fault law more liberally. These days, courts don't investigate the marital breakdown very much, and divorces are granted for almost any reason. As a result, the end-of-marriage issue is seldom contested in divorces any more.

Glossary

Uncontested divorce–divorce where spouses agree on all the divorce issues.

No-fault divorce–all Michigan divorces, whether contested or uncontested, are no-fault divorces since they must use no-fault grounds.

Property Division

Years ago, divorce property division was little more than divvying up pots, pans and clothing. But today a lot more may be at stake. *Forbes* magazine recently listed the women receiving the largest divorce property divisions.

Topping the list were Anne Bass, ex-wife of real estate magnate Sid Bass ($200 million), Frances Lear, who divorced Norman Lear, producer of *All in the Family* and *Maude*, ($112 million), and actress Amy Irving, ex-wife of filmmaker Steven Spielberg ($100 million).

What all these divorces have in common is that they happened in either Texas or California, which are community property states. In these states, marriage is considered an equal financial partnership, so most property acquired during a marriage belongs to the spouses equally, regardless of which spouse earned or owned it. And when a marriage ends—by death or divorce—each spouse gets one-half of the marital property.

Only nine states, mostly in the South and West, have community property. The rest, including Michigan, have a different system of property ownership and division. At one time, Michigan divided property during divorce strictly according to ownership: Each spouse got whatever they owned. This system was simple and neat, but it discriminated against wives because husbands usually owned most property.

Accused of unfairness, Michigan adopted an equitable distribution system of property division in divorce cases. Like community property law, equitable distribution recognizes that marriage is a financial partnership, giving each spouse a share of the property regardless of ownership.

Despite that similarity, community property and equitable distribution divide property very differently. Spouses always get equal shares of community property. In equitable distribution, the shares can be equal or unequal. All the law asks is that the division be "just and reasonable" or "equitable" under the circumstances.

The flexibility of equitable distribution shows up in court decisions. For example, in Michigan divorces wives have gotten as much as 90% or as little as 10% of the property. Under equitable distribution, such lopsided divisions are permissible if justified by the facts of the case. Nevertheless, these are exceptional cases. In the vast majority of divorces, a 50-50 split, or something close to it, is the equitable division.

Court-Ordered Property Division

When spouses wrangle over property, the court must divide it for them during a trial. According to equitable distribution, the division must be "just and reasonable" or "equitable." But since these general principles don't give enough guidance, courts have developed nine specific factors for property division:

- duration of the marriage
- contribution of the parties to the marital estate
- age of the parties
- health of the parties
- life status of the parties
- necessities and circumstances of the parties
- earning abilities of the parties
- past relations and conduct of the parties
- general principles of equity

In many states, property divisions are based solely on economic factors. If fault is taken into account, it's only to the extent that fault has had an impact on the property. For example, California ignores fault in property divisions except when one spouse has squandered the community property. In that case of "economic fault," the other spouse gets a greater share of the property.

Most of Michigan's property division factors are also economic. But fault creeps into divorce when the property division is contested through the "past relations and conduct of the parties" factor. And in Michigan, this fault isn't confined to misuse of property. It can include almost any type of marital misconduct, no matter how embarrassing or lurid.

Since equitable distribution is designed to be flexible, courts can weigh the property division factors much as they wish. They can focus on the important factors in the case, while disregarding others that don't apply. Courts may also consider other things through the catch-all "general principles of equity" factor.

Courts can avoid all that if the parties have a prenuptial agreement, since the agreement will normally control the division of property. Prenuptial agreements (also called antenuptial agreements or marital contracts) are contracts between spouses-to-be spelling out how property shall be divided when the marriage ends by death or divorce.

Michigan courts weren't always willing to use prenuptial agreements during divorce. For years, they refused to enforce these agreements believing that they encouraged divorce. But in 1991, the Michigan Court of Appeals reversed that rule and decided that prenuptial agreements are enforceable when: 1) the agreement was fairly entered into before the marriage 2) the agreement itself was fair at the time it was signed 3) facts and circumstances haven't changed enough since the agreement was signed that would make it unfair to enforce the agreement.

Uncontested Property Division

Before you and your spouse agree on a property division, you must know the extent and value of your property. "Can I Get a Fair Property Division?" on page 31 has important information about that. It tells which property is divisible in a divorce, and how to value it.

After you agree on a property division, the court should approve it because you have more control over property division than other divorce issues. If you happen to have a prenuptial agreement dealing with divorce, you should be able to use it to divide your property, unless the agreement is "unfair" (see above for the fairness requirements for prenuptial agreements). Whatever you decide about property division, see "Property Division Provisions" on page 153 in Appendix F for information about providing for and carrying out the division.

Alimony

From the start, American courts awarded support in the form of alimony to wives. In 1641, just two years after the first American divorce, Massachusetts Bay Colony passed a law giving wives a right to alimony.

During this era, courts regarded alimony as wife-support, and husbands never got it. But in the 1960s, states revised their alimony laws to make it payable to either men or women. Michigan amended its alimony law in 1970 to permit alimony for men.

Since then, there have been some well-publicized cases of women paying alimony to men. Actresses Jane Seymour and Roseanne Barr reportedly paid their former husbands alimony. And even among the less famous, men are receiving alimony more often as women achieve financial parity with men. But typically, men are the alimony payers and women are the recipients.

Despite all the attention it gets, alimony has never been very common. At the beginning of this century, alimony was awarded in a scant 9.3% of divorces. Although exact figures are hard to come by, that percentage seems to have increased during the next 50 years. One study of California divorces in 1968 found that wives received alimony in 20% of divorces. But by 1975, only 14% of divorce cases included alimony.

As the number of alimony orders declined, the duration of alimony also shrank. Years ago, alimony was usually an open-ended award which continued indefinitely until the wife remarried or died. Nowadays, alimony is likely to be for a limited time—maybe a year or two—to help the recipient get back on his/her feet after divorce. This kind of short-term alimony is sometimes referred to as rehabilitative or transitional alimony.

In Michigan, alimony can be paid during a divorce or afterward. Alimony during a divorce is available as preliminary relief, but only through a temporary order issued after a motion and hearing. See "Do I Need 'Preliminary Relief'?" on page 37 for more about preliminary alimony.

Whether or not preliminary alimony has been ordered, alimony can be granted in the Judgment of Divorce at the end of the divorce. In most cases, alimony takes the form of cash payments payable periodically.

These payments won't last forever because divorce judgments invariably make alimony subject to conditions ending it. These conditions are negotiable, but most judgments contain several of the following:

Death. Alimony is almost always terminated when the recipient dies (as explained below, there are sound tax reasons for making such a provision). Alimony doesn't automatically end when the payer dies, and it can survive and become a debt of his/her estate. Nevertheless, judgments often terminate alimony when payers die.

Remarriage. Alimony often ends when the recipient remarries, but seldom ends if the payer remarries.

Cohabitation. To prevent recipients from choosing cohabitation over remarriage as a way to keep alimony, the alimony may end if the recipient cohabitates with a member of the opposite sex.

Date. Alimony may end on a specific date.

Modification. In Michigan, true alimony has customarily been open to modification when there has been a change in the parties' circumstances. A modification could result in an increase, decrease or even termination of the alimony.

Michigan law does allow divorce parties to designate alimony as non-modifiable. However, this has to be done carefully in a negotiated divorce settlement; you can't do it in an uncontested divorce without input from the defendant. Thus, all alimony described in this book remains modifiable.

Types of Alimony

Alimony is a slippery word because Michigan divorce law, federal tax law and federal bankruptcy law all define alimony differently. Adding to complications, Michigan court rules use the phrase "spousal support" instead of alimony. Because of this, the forms in this book also use spousal support to mean alimony, although the text will use the familiar term alimony.

Michigan divorce law regards as alimony any divorce-related payments of money or other property from one (ex)spouse to the other for purposes of support. As explained before, alimony usually takes the form of cash payments paid periodically (weekly, monthly, etc.). There is another kind of so-called alimony, alimony-in-gross, which is often paid in several lump-sum payments. Despite its name, alimony-in-gross is really division of a liquid asset: money. Thus, alimony-in-gross is really property division and not true alimony.

Federal law has its own rules for defining alimony. The federal tax law generally disregards what parties call their payments. Instead, it considers support payments as alimony if they are:

• paid in cash (including checks or money orders)
• made to a spouse or to someone on his/her behalf

- made in a divorce document (such as a divorce order or judgment)
- made when the spouses are living apart (subject to several exceptions, including payment of temporary alimony)
- end on the death of the recipient-spouse
- not provided as child support
- not designated as something other than alimony

These tax rules are important because payments that qualify as alimony get special tax treatment. The payments are deductible by the payer and counted as income for the recipient.

Federal bankruptcy law has yet another definition of alimony. According to bankruptcy law, support payments qualify as alimony if they are: 1) intended by the parties as alimony 2) actually used for support 3) a reasonable amount of support. When payments are treated as alimony under bankruptcy law, they're protected from elimination or discharge during a bankruptcy of the payer. If the payments don't qualify as alimony, the payer can sometimes discharge them in bankruptcy.

Payment of Alimony

Like child support, alimony is normally paid by immediate income withholding to the state disbursement unit (SDU). But it's possible set up other payment methods, and have alimony paid to the SDU without immediate income withholding or even directly to the payee. See "Choosing an Alimony Payment Method" on page 164 for more about these and other payment options.

Court-Ordered Alimony

When spouses contest the issue of alimony, the court must decide the issue in a trial. To determine whether alimony is payable, the court considers the following factors:

- length of the marriage
- ability of the parties to work
- source of and amount of property awarded to the parties
- age of the parties
- ability of the parties to pay alimony
- present situation of the parties
- needs of the parties
- health of the parties
- prior standard of living of the parties and whether either is responsible for the support of others
- past relations and conduct of the parties
- general principles of equity

Like property division, the procedure for deciding alimony is flexible, so a court may apply these factors as it chooses. It can weigh the factors unequally, disregard ones that don't apply or add others that seem important through the catch-all "general principles of equity" factor.

Most of the alimony factors are economic. That makes sense because what alimony is really about is the need of one spouse for support and the ability of the other to pay it. But fault can creep in through the "past relations and conduct of the parties" factor. As with property division, fault in contested alimony cases may include almost any evidence of marital misconduct.

After a court decides that alimony is due, it must then determine the amount. In Michigan, there are no uniform alimony guidelines as there are for child support. So most judges set alimony on a case-by-case basis using the following factors:

- length of the marriage
- contributions of the parties to the joint estate
- age and health of the parties
- parties' stations in life
- necessities of the parties
- earning ability of the parties

In 1983, Washtenaw County rejected the case-by-case approach and adopted an alimony formula. It judges the strength of an alimony claim (length of the marriage, age, income and job skills are the most important factors), adjusts the claim for other factors and then provides for a mathematical computation of alimony. Recently, other counties have begun using Washtenaw's formula or adaptations of it. This suggests a need for a uniform state-wide formula, which may be developed in the future.

Uncontested Alimony

Since alimony isn't ordered in most divorces, divorce judgments usually waive (surrender) alimony. Sometimes it's possible to reserve alimony, allowing you to ask for it after the divorce. Or you and your spouse can agree to have alimony granted by including an alimony order in your divorce judgment.

"Alimony Provisions" on page 162 in Appendix F has more information about all those methods of dealing with alimony. It also includes two basic alimony orders for short- and long-term periodic alimony, which you can adapt to your situation.

Other Divorce Issues

Ending the marriage, property division and alimony aren't the only divorce issues. But any other divorce issues are relatively minor and seldom contested.

Name change for women is one such minor issue. After a divorce, women often want to drop their married names and resume maiden or former names. For them, Michigan law offers two name change methods: 1) common law name change by usage 2) court-ordered name change from: (a) the court when the divorce is granted (b) a separate name change case later.

The usage method is the easiest because all you do is choose a new name and begin using it regularly. No court order is necessary. The name change is legal as long as you're not adopting a new name for a fraudulent or improper purpose.

The trouble with the usage method is that it's no longer very effective. These days, with the general anxiety about security and special concern about identity theft, authorities want official proof of name changes; informal name changes aren't acceptable any more. As a result, most women choose formal court-ordered name changes.

It's easy for a woman to change her name during divorce. When the divorce is final, the court can allow the wife, whether she is plaintiff or defendant, to adopt a different surname (last name). She may resume a maiden or former name, or choose any other surname. The only restriction is that the name change mustn't be sought with "any fraudulent or evil intent" (to avoid past debts, hide from law enforcement officials, etc.). The divorce papers in this book have provisions for women to ask for and receive name changes.

Some women who ultimately want to change their names aren't ready for name changes during divorce. For personal or other reasons, they may want to keep their married names for a while, and then change later.

Women seeking name changes post-divorce must file separate name change cases. Before filing, they must satisfy a one-year county residency requirement. They must be fingerprinted by the police and submit to a criminal background check. After publishing a legal notice in the newspaper, they must attend a court hearing to get the name change.

Needless to say, this procedure takes much more effort than a divorce name change. That's why most women, if they have a choice, choose a name change during divorce.

Name change at divorce is seldom an issue for men, because men don't customarily change their names at marriage. However, today some men add their wives' surnames to their own, by hyphenation, at marriage, and may then want to drop the addition at divorce.

Michigan divorce law isn't very helpful for men in this predicament. The law has no provision for male name changes during divorce. To change their names at divorce, men must do it by custom and usage under the common law method, of file a separate name change case, outside of divorce, to get a formal a court-ordered name change.

PART III: Doing an Uncontested Divorce Yourself

Most uncontested divorces go smoothly. But divorce remains a difficult legal procedure, and can sometimes get complicated. There may be a problem with jurisdiction, trouble serving the divorce papers, difficulty dividing the property or the danger of spouse abuse. All these problems and more can make your divorce—although it's uncontested—too difficult for you to do yourself.

Am I Married?

It may seem silly, but the first thing you should do before a divorce is make sure you are really married. If you discover that you aren't married, you won't need a divorce to split up.

The legality of a marriage is judged by the law of where it began, not where it ends. If you were married in Michigan, you look at Michigan marriage law. Those married out of state must consider the marriage law of that place.

Michigan authorizes two types of marriage: 1) ceremonial marriage, performed by most clergymen and some government officials 2) secret marriage, a rather obscure form of marriage before a probate judge for the benefit of: (a) people with a good reason to keep their marriage secret (b) children under the age of 16 in certain circumstances. Other states have different types of ceremonial marriage, which are valid in Michigan.

Most states have abolished common law marriage, in which couples informally agree to live together as husband and wife. However, many states had it in the past. Michigan recognized common law marriage until January

1, 1957. Today, only the District of Columbia and the following states permit common law marriage:

- Alabama
- Colorado
- Iowa
- Kansas
- Montana

- Pennsylvania
- Rhode Island
- South Carolina
- Texas
- Utah

If your common law marriage began in one of these states, it's legal in Michigan. Or if it began in Michigan before January 1, 1957, or in other states while they recognized the institution, it's also valid here.

If you doubt whether you are really married, check with the official of the office where you believe your marriage license is filed. In Michigan, that official is the county clerk who issued the license to you; in other states it might be someone else.

Another way to trace marriage records is through a state vital records office. Every state has an office that compiles records of marriages, divorces, births and deaths. By writing to the vital records office of the state in which you think you were married, you can get a copy of your marriage license, if one exists.

After you confirm that you are married, you should also make sure that your marriage hasn't already ended by divorce or annulment. Unlike common law marriage, there is no such thing as informal "common law" divorce. So despite what some people think, tearing up your marriage license, giving back wedding rings, etc. will not make you divorced. Therefore, any divorce that your spouse may have gotten must have been court-ordered.

If you think that you may have been involved in a prior divorce, investigate and see whether a divorce judgment (also known as a decree or order in some states) was ever issued in the case. The court where the divorce was filed will have record of the judgment. If you don't have much information about the divorce, use the procedure described above to contact the vital records office of the state where the divorce was filed. It should have a record of the divorce judgment, if in fact one was issued.

Naturally, your spouse's death also ends your marriage. You might not know about this if you've separated from your spouse and remained out of touch. If you suspect that your spouse has died, you can confirm that by checking to see if a death certificate was filed. In Michigan, death certificates are filed with the county clerk of the place of death. If you don't know the county, use the state vital records office. A quicker way to check on the death of anyone is through the Social Security Administration's (SSA) death index.

More Information

To obtain Michigan marriage, divorce and death records, contact Michigan's vital records office:

Department of Community Health
Division for Vital Records and Health Studies
P.O. Box 30195
Lansing, MI 48909
(517) 335-8496

To find vital records offices in other states, order the booklet "Where to Write for Vital Records" (#107L), by sending a $4.25 check (payable to "Superintendent of Documents"), to:

R. Woods
CIC - 01A
P.O. Box 100
Pueblo, CO 81002

You can also order this booklet with a credit card by calling (888) 878-3256. Or you can read or print the booklet at www.pueblo.gsa.gov.

You can also find state vital records through www.vitalrec.com.

The SSA's death index lists deceased people whose survivors have received social security death benefits. Not everyone applies for or receives these benefits, so the index isn't 100% complete, but it's a good place to start.

To use the index, call the SSA at (800) 772-1213.

The index is also available at www.ancestry.com for a fee.

It's also possible to have your spouse legally declared dead after a long disappearance. Like most states, Michigan has an Enoch Arden law (so called after the shipwrecked sailor of the Tennyson poem who returned from ten years at sea to find his wife remarried), which allows a person to be declared dead after seven years of complete absence.

Do I Really Want to End My Marriage?

When you get a divorce, the marriage between you and your spouse is ended finally and irrevocably. This allows each of you to remarry, if you wish. As someone divorce-bound, you're probably well aware of these and other benefits of divorce.

But as you prepare to divorce, don't forget the many advantages of remaining married. Recently, when Vermont lawmakers were debating their controversial same-sex civil union law, legal experts there counted around 300 benefits of marriage offered by state law. Michigan law certainly provides as many or more. All in all, marriage offers many valuable rights, such as: 1) support 2) property rights 3) estate and will rights 4) private benefits 5) public benefits 6) miscellaneous rights.

To be sure, some of these rights can be continued or compensated after a divorce. You can sometimes get postdivorce support in the form of alimony, and your property rights, including rights in retirement plans, can be recovered in the property division of the divorce.

But many marital rights are lost forever by a divorce. After a divorce, you lose all rights to your spouse's estate, including: 1) the right to inherit a share of his/her estate if s/he dies without a will 2) the right to take a minimum share of the estate, if the will slights you 3) dower (an estate that widows have in their husbands' real property) 4) miscellaneous allowances from your deceased spouse's estate. Divorce also automatically revokes all distributions of property and some appointments in your spouse's will which benefit you.

You may also lose valuable private benefits, often provided by an employer, available through your spouse, such as retirement, fringe, life and health plan benefits. There are substitutes for some of these, such as COBRA-provided health care coverage (see "Health Care Coverage" on page 99 for more more about this type of coverage), but never completely and usually at a higher cost.

More Information

On divorce and social security, get "A Woman's Guide to Social Security" from your local social security office.

See "Can I Get A Fair Property Division?" on page 31 for resources about retirement benefits.

Good information about these and other topics:

Divorce & Money, 4th ed., Violet Woodhouse and Dale Fetherling, Berkeley: Nolo Press, 2002

The Dollars and Sense of Divorce, Judith Briles, et al., Chicago: Dearborn Trade Publishing, 1998

The death of your spouse after your divorce will leave you
without public benefits, such as wrongful death claims or
survivor's benefits from worker's compensation or no-fault
automobile insurance, that you might have enjoyed had you
remained married. What's worse, if you happen to divorce
before the tenth anniversary of your marriage, you may lose the
right to get social security benefits based on your spouse's earnings record.

Divorce also jeopardizes other miscellaneous marital rights
that you may have never thought about. For example, aliens
(noncitizens) can lose entrance or residence rights when they
divorce U.S. citizens. After a divorce, you cannot file a joint
income tax return, and may face a bigger tax bill. Marriage also
entitles you to discounts on airplane tickets, hotels, etc., which
single people don't always enjoy.

After considering all that marriage offers, you may decide
that it isn't so bad after all. If you think that your marriage can be saved, you
may find marriage counseling helpful. Many religious and human service
organizations provide counseling, usually without charge. Private marriage
and family counselors offer similar services. These private counselors charge
fees for their services, but some health plans pay for the cost.

Is Divorce the Best Way to End My Marriage?

Divorce isn't the only cure for a bad marriage. By declaring a marriage
nonexistent, an annulment also ends the marriage. A legal separation—
known as separate maintenance in Michigan—ends a marital relationship,
although the marriage itself is left intact. Like divorce, an annulment or
separate maintenance allows the court to decide the issues of property
division and alimony. Before you choose a divorce, consider whether an
annulment or separate maintenance might be better for you.

Annulment

Many people don't really understand annulment. For one thing, they often
confuse legal annulments with religious annulments. Legal annulments are
granted by courts of law, and affect one's legal rights. Some religious
denominations, notably the Roman Catholic Church, offer religious annulments. These end marriages in the eyes in the church, restoring various
religious privileges. A religious annulment is obtained from the religious
organization and has absolutely no effect on legal rights.

Another misunderstanding about annulments is that they are routinely
available for spouses who have been married for a short time and simply
want to "call the whole thing off." The fact is, the length of a marriage is
often insignificant: A marriage of a few days may not be annullable, just as
a marriage of many years can be annulled. The real distinction between
divorce and annulment is that a divorce ends a valid marriage, while an

annulment is a legal declaration that no marriage ever existed because of a serious legal defect in the marriage at the time it was performed.

Like most states, Michigan presumes that marriages are legally valid. As a result, minor legal defects in a marriage, such as irregularities in the marriage ceremony, lack of authority of the person who performed the ceremony, etc., are excusable. But if the legal defect is serious, the marriage is subject to annulment. In Michigan, the serious legal defects providing grounds for an annulment concern whether the spouses: 1) had the legal capacity to marry 2) properly consented to marriage.*

Glossary
Divorce–legal procedure that ends a marriage.
Annulment–says that a marriage is legally defective and never really existed.
Separate maintenance–like a legal separation, allowing the spouses to live apart with marriage still intact.

Legal capacity. One must satisfy several requirements to marry in Michigan. If a spouse failed to meet any of these requirements when the marriage was performed, the spouse lacked the legal capacity for marriage. This defect can provide grounds for annulment:

¶ *Bigamy.* A spouse marries while already married to someone else.

¶ *Incest.* The spouses are related too closely by blood (you cannot marry a parent, child, grandchild, grandparent, brother or sister, aunt or uncle, niece or nephew or first cousin) or marriage (a stepparent, stepchild, stepgrandchild, son- or daughter-in-law, father- or mother-in-law, spouse of a grandchild or grandparent-in-law are all not marriageable).

¶ *Same-sex marriage.* Michigan doesn't permit same-sex marriage, or recognize same-sex marriages from other states.

¶ *Underage.* Eighteen is the age of consent to marry in Michigan. Men and women 16-18 can marry if they obtain the proper parental consent. Under some circumstances, children under 16 can marry with parental consent in a secret marriage in probate court. Anyone who marries while underage and/or without the proper parental consent, lacks the legal capacity to marry.

¶ *Mental incompetency.* Mental incompetency of a spouse at the time of a marriage is an additional legal incapacity. Onset of mental incompetency after marriage doesn't affect the marriage.

¶ *Physical incapacity.* Sterility and some kinds of sexual dysfunction, which exist at the time of the marriage, are also recognized as incapacities.

---

* As mentioned before, the legality of a marriage is judged by the law of the state where it began. These annulment grounds apply to Michigan marriages only. There may be different annulment grounds for out-of-state marriages.

Consent. According to Michigan law, both spouses must give proper consent to their marriage. If a spouse's consent is absent or defective, for any of the reasons below, the marriage may be annulled:

¶ *Force.* A spouse's consent to the marriage is obtained forcibly. Ordinarily, the force must be the use or threat of physical force, but in some cases extreme psychological duress will qualify as force.

¶ *Intoxication.* A spouse's consent to the marriage might be defective if s/he is under the influence of alcohol or drugs when the marriage is performed.

¶ *Fraud.* Fraud is a misrepresentation that causes someone to do something. If fraud is used to obtain consent to a marriage, the fraud can invalidate the marriage. Michigan law is clear that the fraud must affect an essential part of the marriage. For example, a spouse's misrepresentation about his/her ability to have or want children, or about an intention to engage in cohabitation or sexual relations, may be important enough to annul the marriage. But misrepresentations by a spouse about character, wealth, family background or premarital life don't provide fraud grounds for an annulment.

¶ *Sham marriage.* Even when consent to a marriage is given voluntarily and knowingly, the consent might be defective if it wasn't seriously intended. Marriages based on such false consent are regarded as sham marriages, making them subject to annulment. An example of a sham marriage is a marriage by an alien (noncitizen) who marries a U.S. citizen solely to obtain permanent residence in this country. In that case, the alien's marriage may appear to be proper, but it is really nothing more than a ruse to obtain residence in this country.

If you possess any of these grounds for annulment, you may be able to end your marriage by annulment. Or you can disregard the annulment grounds, file for divorce and end your marriage that way. Which is the better choice?

There is no simple answer to this question because divorces closely resemble annulments. Both procedures end marriages and free spouses to remarry. They both divide property. But alimony, especially long-term alimony, is difficult to get in an annulment.

An annulment may be quicker than a divorce. Annulments don't have waiting periods as divorces do (see "How Long Will My Divorce Take?" on page 28 for information about divorce waiting periods). And there are no state or county residence requirements for annulments as there are in divorce cases (see "Can I Get a Divorce in Michigan?" and "Can I File the Divorce in My County?" on pages 24-26 for more on state and county divorce residence requirements).

On the other hand, the grounds for annulment are harder to prove and easier to defend against than the no-fault divorce grounds. What's worse, most annulment grounds are based on fault. This means that an annulment can be messy, like divorce was under the old fault law.

If you believe that you have grounds for an annulment and cannot decide whether to file for divorce or annulment, talk with a lawyer about which procedure to use. Act quickly because it's possible to lose annulment grounds by waiting too long. If you decide to seek an annulment, have the lawyer represent you because this book doesn't have instructions or forms for annulment.

Separation

Unlike divorce or annulment, separation doesn't end a marriage. It merely ends the marital relationship between the spouses, leaving the marriage itself intact. Despite that fact, there may be sound reasons for choosing separation over divorce or annulment.

Years ago, people often separated to avoid the social stigma of divorce. With divorce more common now, this stigma has faded. Nevertheless, some people may still want to separate and remain married for social or religious reasons.

Some couples choose separation for more practical reasons. As explained before, spouses can lose valuable marital rights when their marriage ends. Since separation doesn't break the legal bond of marriage, it preserves these marital rights. With this in mind, spouses may decide to separate temporarily, and divorce later when losing these rights isn't so important. For example, spouses married eight or nine years might agree to separate for a few years, and then divorce, so they can qualify for social security benefits based on each other's earnings under the ten-year rule mentioned above. Or they may remain married to preserve benefits like health plan coverage.

Informal Separation

You don't need to go to court to separate. As a matter of fact, spouses can separate informally and live apart indefinitely. Separated spouses usually work out arrangements for property division and sometimes alimony. To avoid disputes, some estranged spouses enter into written separation or settlement agreements. These agreements spell out how property division and alimony are handled during the separation. In addition, the agreement can settle these issues for any divorce following the separation.

An informal separation—even one with a written separation agreement—is difficult to maintain. If the spouses disagree about something, they have no place to resolve their dispute. As a result, some separated spouses seek a formal, court-ordered separation, which is popularly known as a legal separation.

Legal Separation: Separate Maintenance

Michigan law provides for a special type of legal separation called separate maintenance. Separate maintenance doesn't end the marriage. But it settles the issues of property division and alimony while the spouses live apart.

The procedure for getting a separate maintenance is like that for a divorce. Even the same no-fault grounds are used. Despite the resemblance, it's much harder to get a separate maintenance because Michigan law allows a defendant in a separate maintenance case to ask for a divorce instead. After the request, the court must grant a divorce if the marriage is broken. Therefore, it's impossible to get a separate maintenance without the approval of the other spouse. All this makes separate maintenance difficult, so see a lawyer if you want one.

Can I Get a Divorce in Michigan?

After deciding that a divorce is what you want, you must then determine whether you can get one in Michigan. Not everyone is entitled to divorce in Michigan. To get a divorce in this state, Michigan courts must have jurisdiction to hear your divorce case. Jurisdiction is based on the residences of you and your spouse.

Residence

Residence is vital to your case as the basis for jurisdiction. But what is it really? Residence has different legal meanings. For the purposes of divorce, residence means your permanent home, or the place you intend to stay.

Glossary

Plaintiff–spouse who files for divorce.

Defendant–spouse against whom divorce is filed.

Jurisdiction–power of a court to decide a divorce case.

Venue—in divorce cases, the correct county for divorce-filing.

Long-time residents of Michigan don't have to worry about residence. But if you've moved to the state recently, you can establish residence by: 1) registering to vote here 2) getting a Michigan driver's license 3) owning property in the state (it's even better if you file for a homestead property tax exemption at your Michigan address) 4) working and filing income tax returns here.

Once established in Michigan, residence isn't lost by temporary absences out of state, such as vacations or business trips. Nor is it disturbed by leaving the state under military or government orders. For example, a resident of Michigan who enters the U.S. military or foreign service remains a Michigan resident during active duty wherever assigned.

Residence may be important for the purposes of jurisdiction before you file a divorce, but it's much less important afterward. In fact, after you file the divorce you or your spouse can move anywhere—in or outside Michigan—without losing jurisdiction for your divorce.

Divorce Jurisdiction

Michigan divorce jurisdiction is based on the past and present residences of the spouses. These residences determine whether there is either full or limited jurisdiction for the case. A court can take full jurisdiction when at least the defendant-spouse is residing in Michigan (the plaintiff-spouse may be residing here as well), or when the spouses resided together in Michigan

Michigan Divorce Jurisdiction

	Defendant is a Michigan resident (and has been for at least 180 days immediately before the divorce is filed)	Defendant once resided with plaintiff in Michigan during their marriage, then moved out of state	Defendant never resided with plaintiff in Michigan during their marriage
Plaintiff is a Michigan resident (and has been for at least 180 days immediately before the divorce is filed)	Full jurisdiction immediately*	Full jurisdiction immediately**	Limited jurisdiction immediately**
Plaintiff once resided with defendant in Michigan during their marriage, then moved out of state	Full jurisdiction immediately	No jurisdiction until plaintiff (or defendant) moves back to Michigan and has resided here at least 180 days immediately before the divorce is filed, then full jurisdiction**	
Plaintiff never resided with defendant in Michigan during their marriage	Full jurisdiction immediately		No jurisdiction until plaintiff (or defendant) moves to Michigan and has resided here at least 180 days immediately before the divorce is filed, then only limited jurisdiction**

* In fact, either plaintiff or defendant can satisfy the 180-day residence requirement by having resided in Michigan at least 180 days immediately before the divorce is filed.

** Full jurisdiction can also be obtained on a nonresident defendant by serving him/her while present in Michigan, such as during a visit to the state.

at some time during their marriage. Limited jurisdiction exists when only the plaintiff-spouse resides in Michigan and the defendant never resided here with him/her during their marriage.

Like other states, Michigan also imposes a residence requirement on divorce to discourage migratory divorce. In Michigan, the residence period is 180 days. The chart above depicts Michigan divorce jurisdiction with the residence requirement added.

The concept of jurisdiction is difficult, but it's important because it determines how much of your case the court can decide. As explained in Part II, divorce is divisible into several issues: end-of-marriage, property division and alimony. For reasons that are too complicated to explain here, certain divorce issues may need a particular type of jurisdiction. For example, property division and alimony require full jurisdiction, while ending a marriage can use either limited or full jurisdiction.

When a court has full jurisdiction, it can do a divorce completely. It can end the marriage, divide the property and award alimony. With only limited jurisdiction, a court can end the marriage, but it cannot decide property division or alimony.

Divorces with minor children almost always require full jurisdiction. But divorces without minor children can sometimes get by with limited jurisdiction. If you have little property, and don't seek alimony, limited jurisdiction may be enough. If not, contact a lawyer to see about getting full Michigan jurisdiction or filing for divorce in the defendant's state.

Can I File the Divorce in My County?

Assuming Michigan courts have some type of jurisdiction for your divorce, you must then file in the Michigan county with proper venue. In divorce cases, venue exists in the county where either you or your spouse has resided at least 10 days immediately before the divorce is filed. Incidentally, residence for venue purposes is a place of permanent habitation, just as it is for jurisdiction.

Naturally, when you both reside in the same county, the divorce must be filed there. But when you reside in different Michigan counties, venue is proper in either county. For the sake of convenience, most people choose to file in their own counties.

If the defendant resides out of state, venue will be in the Michigan county where the plaintiff resides. In those rare cases with out-of-state plaintiffs, venue will be in the Michigan county where the defendant resides.

What If My Spouse and I File for Divorce at the Same Time?

This is the dueling divorces problem: You and your spouse file for divorce around the same time, perhaps even before the divorce papers are served on each other. If both cases were filed in Michigan, the one filed first has priority and the later one must be dismissed (to dismiss the second case, see Appendix E about voluntary dismissal of divorce cases).

When the divorces are filed in different states, the situation is a little more complicated. If both states have full jurisdiction, the first case filed usually has priority. But if only one state has full jurisdiction, that state can do the divorce completely and its case should be the one to go forward.

Can My Spouse Be Served with the Divorce Papers?

Regardless of the type of jurisdiction for a divorce, the defendant must get notice of the divorce. Like other lawsuits, notice in divorce cases is provided by serving the initial divorce papers on defendants. Service is explained in detail in Chapter 2.

At this point, you should know that service is easy and cheap if your spouse is available to receive the divorce papers. In that case, you can obtain service by any of three methods: 1) acknowledgment 2) mail 3) delivery. It doesn't matter where your spouse lives, because these service methods can be used anywhere in or outside Michigan.

Service can be difficult if a defendant is elusive (you know where the defendant is, but s/he is eluding or avoiding you). It's even more difficult if the defendant has disappeared (you don't know the whereabouts of the defendant). Luckily, the court rules provide for forms of alternate service to give hard-to-find defendants some type of notice (Appendix B has more about obtaining alternate service on elusive or disappeared defendants).

Thanks to this wide choice of service methods, you can be confident that when there is jurisdiction for your divorce there will be a way to serve the defendant.

What If My Spouse or I Am Imprisoned?

Incarceration of a spouse naturally puts a great strain on a marriage. If the marriage should break, the imprisonment also creates special problems for the divorce, whether the prisoner is plaintiff or defendant.

Divorce by an Imprisoned Plaintiff

Before filing, an imprisoned plaintiff must choose the correct county for filing. Choice of county is called venue and is controlled by the county residence of the divorce parties.

Prisoners are subject to special residence rules for venue. According to Michigan law, prisoners are presumed to remain residents of the county they resided in immediately before imprisonment. However, prisoners can become residents of the county of imprisonment if they can prove that they intend to reside there after release. Keep these residence rules in mind as you choose venue as directed in "Can I File the Divorce in My County?" above.

Prisoners shouldn't have any difficulty serving their non-institutionalized spouses with divorce papers. The three regular methods of service (acknowledgment, mail, delivery), plus alternate service methods, are available to prisoners. Service by mail is probably easiest and cheapest. All these service methods and rules are explained in "Service" on page 67.

Plaintiff-prisoners do face a special problem at the end of divorce, during the final hearing. Ordinarily, divorce plaintiffs must appear personally in court and give some brief testimony for the Judgment of Divorce. To satisfy the court appearance requirement, some counties transport prisoners to court for final hearings in divorce. But transportation is expensive, especially for counties with large prison populations.

As an alternative, many counties allow and encourage prisoners to give their testimony in written or electronic form. The court rules permit this because they excuse court appearances in exceptional cases. Prisoners

> ## More Information
>
> About divorce problems for prisoners, including giving final hearing testimony from prison, contact:
>
> **Prison Legal Services of Michigan**
> SPSM
> 3855 Cooper St.
> Jackson, MI 49201
> (517) 780-6639

should contact prison legal services for help with giving final hearing testimony without a court appearance.

Filing against a Defendant-Prisoner

More Information

To locate a prison inmate for service and/or obtain the inmate's prisoner identification number, use a prison locator service.

Michigan's locator service can be reached at (517) 335-7570.

For prisoners in other state prisons, see the Johnson and Knox book cited on page 113. It lists all the states' prison locator services.

The federal prison locator is available at (202) 307-3126.

There are fewer problems in a divorce against an incarcerated defendant. Before filing, the plaintiff must consider the venue rules while choosing where to file (see "Can I File the Divorce in My County?" on page 26 for more about venue). Typically, plaintiffs file in their home counties, so the residence of a defendant-prisoner isn't an issue. But if you want to file where a defendant-prisoner resides, see the section above about how the residence of prisoners is established.

Probably the best way to serve a defendant in prison is by mail. Service by mail is described in "Service" on page 67, along with the other service methods. When your service-helper mails the service papers to the defendant, make sure the defendant's prisoner identification number appears next to the defendant's name in the address on the envelope. Many prisons require this number for delivery of mail to inmates. If the defendant refuses to take and sign for the mailing, you can always use service by delivery, through the sheriff's office in the county where the prison is located.

What If My Spouse or I Am in the Military?

Military service adds both practical and legal problems to a divorce. As a practical matter, it may be difficult to find and serve papers on a defendant-servicemember stationed at a faraway military base. There are also state and federal military relief laws protecting active-duty servicemembers from hard-to-handle lawsuits. The federal law, the Soldiers' and Sailors' Civil Relief Act of 1940 (SSCRA), is an especially stiff challenge when the servicemember is a defendant who is uncooperative or unresponsive.

Appendix D has complete information about dealing with military servicemembers whether as divorce plaintiffs or defendants.

How Long Will My Divorce Take?

Uncontested divorces take longer to complete than most uncontested lawsuits because Michigan law imposes two statutory waiting periods on divorces:

- 60 days in cases without minor children
- six months in cases with minor children

The waiting periods serve to delay divorces. The chief reason for the delay is to give the parties a chance to cool off, and possibly reconcile, after the heat of the divorce filing has passed.

In your case, the 60-day statutory waiting period applies. This means that at least 60 days must elapse between the day you file your divorce and the day you finish it in court at the final hearing.

In addition to the statutory waiting period, there may also be unpredictable court-caused delays. Some courts are very busy and may not be able to hear your divorce immediately after the statutory waiting period expires. As a result, your divorce will take at least 60 days, and maybe a while longer if the court is busy.

How Much Will My Divorce Cost?

Doing your own divorce saves you lawyer fees, but not the court fees of the case. These court fees are due in all divorces—with or without lawyers. The court fees for uncontested divorces without minor children include the following items:

Filing fee. The fee for filing a divorce is $150.

Service fee. You can expect to pay $0-30 to have the divorce papers served. The amount of the service fee depends on the method of service you use. Service by acknowledgment is usually available for free. Service by mail is around $8. Service by delivery is usually $16-30. If you use a sheriff for service by delivery, the sheriff charges a $16 fee, plus mileage (billed at the current state government rate) to and from the defendant. Commercial process servers' fees for service by delivery may be slightly higher.

Motion fee. You must pay a $20 fee whenever you file a motion. You probably won't need to file any motions in your uncontested divorce case, unless you have to ask for something extraordinary, like alternate service.

Excluding a service fee, your court fees should be $150 (the current filing fee). Add to that a service fee, which depends on the method of service you choose.

Thanks to a landmark U.S. Supreme Court decision, poor people don't have to pay these court fees. In *Boddie v. Connecticut,* the supreme court decided that states must give everyone access to divorce, since they alone have the power to grant divorces. This means that those who can't afford divorce court fees are entitled to exemptions from payment. After the *Boddie* decision in 1971, Michigan adopted fee exemption rules for all types of cases, including divorce. See Appendix A for information about qualifying and applying for a fee exemption.

Divorce Children

	Children included in divorce	Comments/exceptions
Children born during plaintiff's and defendant's current marriage	Yes	But paternity of children born during a marriage can be disproved by strong evidence that the father is not really the father. If paternity is disproved, the child would usually not be included in the divorce.
Unborn children of the marriage	Yes	
Children born during a previous marriage of plaintiff and defendant	Yes	
Children born to plaintiff and defendant outside of their marriage	Yes, if...	Paternity has been established before the divorce or if it can be proved during the divorce.
Children legally adopted by plaintiff and defendant during their marriage	Yes	
Stepchildren of plaintiff or defendant	No	But if a stepchild was adopted by plaintiff or defendant in a stepparent adoption, it will be a legally adopted child of theirs.
Children given up for adoption, or children over whom both plaintiff and defendant have lost parental rights	No	But if only one parent has lost parental rights, include the children in the divorce and explain the circumstances of the parent's loss of parental rights.

Do I Have Children in My Divorce?

To get a divorce without children, you mustn't have any "divorce children" on the day you file for divorce. Since you obtained this edition of *The Michigan Divorce Book*, you obviously believe that you don't have any divorce children. But before you make this assumption, consider the minor and adult children who make up the divorce children, as defined in the chart above.

The minor children are your children who are under 18 on the day you file for divorce. In some cases, divorce children also includes adult children. According to Michigan law, children between the ages of 18 and 19½ are entitled to support if they are: 1) regularly attending high school on a full-time basis with a reasonable expectation of completing sufficient credits to graduate from high school 2) residing on a full-time basis with the recipient of the support or at an institution. These children must be added to your divorce, and child support must be provided for them. Adult divorce children won't be governed by custody, parenting time or residence of children orders since these stop at age 18.

If you have any of these minor or adult divorce children, you must use a different divorce procedure for cases with minor children. You may be able to use *The Michigan Divorce Book (with minor children)* to do the divorce. See the order form at the front of the book for ordering information.

Can I Get a Fair Property Division?

As explained in "Property Division" on page 9, you are entitled to an equitable division of your property in a divorce. But exactly which property is subject to division?

Some states have rigid schemes for dividing property in divorces. They classify property as either marital-community property or nonmarital-separate property. In these states, only marital-community property is divisible during divorce.

In Michigan, by contrast, divorce property division is more flexible. Everything the spouses own is potentially subject to division. Despite what many people believe, this may include property the spouses brought into their marriage. It can also reach inheritances, will gifts or other gifts (including wedding gifts) received before or during the marriage.

Ordinarily, premarital property, inheritances and gifts are left out of divorce property division, and the spouse who owns this property keeps it. But the nonowner-spouse may claim a share of this property when: 1) s/he or the parties' children need the property for support 2) s/he has contributed to "acquisition, improvement or accumulation" of the property.

Saying that all property is potentially divisible in a divorce begs the question of what is property? Does it include everything the spouses possess, or only those things with a definite market value?

A generation ago, everyone agreed that divisible property was confined to real property (land and buildings) and personal property, such as cash, bank accounts, stocks, bonds, household goods, tools, motor vehicles, etc., with a definite market value. But during the last 20 years, the definition of property has steadily expanded to include almost anything of value, regardless of whether it has a market value. So besides the familiar old property that has always been divided in divorces, there are several types of "new" property that may also be divisible:

Retirement benefits. For years, courts refused to divide retirement benefits, such as pensions, despite the fact that these benefits are often the most valuable thing spouses own. Ultimately, courts realized the unfairness of that position and now nearly all states permit the division of pensions and other retirement benefits.

Today, Michigan courts divide almost any type of retirement benefit provided by public- or private-sector employers, including pensions, 401(k), profit-sharing, employee stock ownership (ESOP) and saving/thrift plans.

More Information

About retirement benefits, send $24.95 for *Your Pension Rights at Divorce: What Women Need to Know* to:

Pension Rights Center
1140 19th St. NW
Suite 602
Washington, DC 20036

Also divisible are individual retirement benefits, such as individual retirement arrangement (IRA), simplified employee pension (SEP) and Keogh (HR-10) plans. The only type of retirement benefit immune from division is social security because it already has a built-in means of paying benefits to divorced spouses (see "Do I Really Want to End My Marriage?" on page 19 for more about obtaining social security off your spouse's earnings record).

Employee benefits. Employees are often eligible for valuable fringe benefits, such as health plan coverage, sick and vacation pay, expense accounts, club memberships, meal allowances, lodging, discounts, etc. Some of these benefits, such as banked sick and vacation pay, have been divided in divorce cases in Michigan.

Life insurance. Life insurance is often overlooked during property division, but it's divisible if it has a cash value. Whole life insurance policies usually have a cash value; term insurance policies ordinarily don't.

Businesses. Businesses, such as a sole proprietorship (one-person business) or an interest in a partnership or a small corporation whose stock is not traded publicly, are also divorce property.

Education. Michigan was one of the first states to include education in divorce property divisions. According to Michigan law, education leading to an *advanced* degree (graduate, law, medicine, etc.) is divisible when the degree was the result of a "concerted family effort." What this means is that the nondegree-spouse contributed financial or other support to the spouse earning the advanced degree. If so, the nondegree-spouse's contribution can be valued and awarded to him/her.

Legal claims. Some legal claims that a spouse has against third parties, such as personal injury or workers' compensation claims, are property that can be divided in divorces. For example, in one Michigan case a husband was awarded $700,000 for a libel claim, and the divorce court ruled that his wife was entitled to about half of the money.

  Spouses may also have legal claims against each other that can be decided in a divorce. At one time, it was impossible for spouses to sue each other for personal injuries. This immunity has recently been abolished and spouses are adding personal injury claims to divorces more often.

Debts. Although it's hard to think of debts as property, they should be weighed during the property division because debts influence the overall fairness of the division.

  Whether your property is old, new or a mixture of both, you must have a good grasp of the extent and value of your property. Otherwise, you and your spouse risk agreeing to an inequitable property division. In all, you should do three things before you agree to a property division: 1) *inventory* your property 2) *value* it 3) find a way to *divide* it.

Inventorying Property

Property division begins with a complete inventory of all the property you and your spouse own. Ordinarily, only property owned when the divorce is filed will be divided. Property transferred before the divorce* or acquired during the divorce is normally left out of the division. So take your inventory just before you file.

As you inventory your property, you may find that you don't know very much about it. In many marriages, one spouse handles the finances, leaving the other spouse in the dark. Luckily, there are several informal ways to get the financial information you need for the inventory.

Start with documents around the house, such as paycheck stubs, bank statements and retirement plan booklets. If you and your spouse have a joint safe deposit box, go through the box. You might find deeds, land contracts, stocks, bonds and life insurance policies hidden there.

Your recent joint personal tax returns, especially any schedules attached to these returns, can reveal valuable information about real property (schedules D and E) bank accounts (schedule B), and businesses (schedules C and F). Likewise, joint business income tax returns have important information about businesses. If you have discarded these returns, you can order copies by submitting Form 4506 to your IRS filing center.

Have you and your spouse applied for a loan recently? If so, you probably prepared a financial statement as part of the loan application. Since federal law makes it a crime to submit false information in the statement, it can be a reliable source of financial information.

If these informal methods fail to give you the financial information you need, there is a formal fact-finding device called discovery. Discovery comes in several forms, including depositions (oral interrogation out of court), interrogatories (written questions) and requests for documents. All these discovery methods are available during divorce to get you the financial information you need. The trouble is, discovery is difficult for nonlawyers to use. If you think you need it, contact a lawyer for help.

Valuing Property

There are many methods of valuing property. Michigan law doesn't say which method must be used, but fair market value seems to be the accepted measure of value.

Fair market value is usually defined as the price property would bring in a sale between a willing buyer and willing seller. When the property is subject to a debt, an adjustment may be necessary. For indebted property, the equity value of the property—its fair market value minus the debt against it—is often used instead of gross fair market value.

---

* But see "Does My Property Need Protection?" on page 36 for how courts can stop a spouse from transferring property to keep it out of the divorce.

To value real property, you can either: 1) compare your property to the sale prices of other similar property sold recently in your neighborhood 2) double the amount of your property's tax assessment, since assessments are usually around 50% of market value.

You should be able to establish the fair market value of most kinds of personal property informally without going to the trouble and expense of getting formal appraisals.

Cash or near-cash assets (bank accounts, certificates of deposit, money market funds, etc.) are worth their present account balances. The value of stocks, corporate bonds and other securities are listed daily in the *Wall Street Journal*. Use the current redemption value for series E/EE U.S. savings bonds. You can value whole life insurance by figuring the cash surrender value on the policy chart, or by asking the insurance company or your insurance agent for this value.

The value of motor vehicles can be obtained from National Automobile Dealer Association (NADA) bluebooks. There are also price guides for stamps, coins, jewelry and antiques. You can estimate the value of household goods and tools by comparing them to similar used items.

If these resources don't provide accurate valuations of your property, you can always get formal appraisals. There are appraisers who are competent to value many types of property and specialists who appraise one type of property. People who buy and sell property, such as automobile or antique dealers, can also give appraisals.

The valuation of some new property, such as retirement benefits and businesses, poses special problems. These things have value, but there is no marketplace in which their value can be fixed. After all, you can't very well sell your pension to someone else. You may be able to sell a small business, but the market is often faulty and you won't get what it's really worth. Despite these problems, there are ways to assign value to new property so it can be divided in divorce cases.

Before you can value retirement benefits, you must know what kind of benefit it is. There are two basic kinds of plans providing retirement benefits:

Defined benefit plan. In a defined benefit plan, or pension plan, the employer promises to pay stipulated benefits at retirement or death. These benefits are paid according to formulas which are usually based on a combination of the employee's age, years of service and earnings.

What an employee with a defined benefit plan has is the employer's promise of benefits; there is no retirement account reserved for the employee. Instead, the employer's retirement contributions (typically only the employer contributes) are pooled in a common fund, and retirement benefits are drawn from the fund as needed.

Most large private- and public-sector employers have defined benefit plans, although some are now discontinuing them in favor of defined contribution plans, especially the popular 401(k) plan.

Other employers have adopted a new kind of defined benefit plan, called a cash balance plan, which resembles a 401(k) plan. In a cash balance plan, employers make hypothetical contributions to employees' retirement "accounts," like defined contribution plans. But in reality, these accounts are merely bookkeeping entries, and all retirement benefits are drawn from a common fund. Thus, a cash balance plan remains a defined benefit plan.

Defined contribution plan. In some ways, a defined contribution plan is the opposite of a defined benefit plan. With a defined contribution plan, the employer's contributions, instead of the retirement benefits, are fixed. Each employee has a separate retirement account earmarked for him/her, to which s/he may contribute. The money in the employee's retirement account is invested (usually by the employer), and any investment income is added to the account. At retirement, benefits are paid from the account as the employee directs.

There are many types of defined contributions plans: 401(k), profit-sharing, ESOP and saving/thrift plans (provided by employers), and IRA, SEP and Keogh (HR-10) plans (individual plans). Typically, small businesses have defined contributions plans, although the giant TIAA-CREF (the Teachers Insurance and Annuity Account-College Retirement Equity Fund), which provides retirement benefits to public school teachers, is a defined contribution plan.

The value of a defined benefit plan lies in the benefits the plan will pay in the future. These future benefits can be reduced to a current lump-sum value, called present value. Figuring present value isn't easy, but an accountant or pension specialist can do it for you. To value a defined contribution plan, you simply take the current account balance. You can get this figure from a recent benefit statement or by requesting it from the retirement plan administrator.

Valuing a business is also difficult. If the business cannot be sold as a going concern, the book value of the business (tangible business assets minus business liabilities) may be used. But if the business is marketable, consider valuing the business by multiplying the average annual net earnings (before taxes) by a multiplier (1, 1½, 2, etc.) customary for that type of business. If you own a business jointly with others, you may have a buy-sell agreement with the co-owners fixing the value of your share, and you can use this value.

Dividing Property

All real property must be divided by separate property division provisions in the divorce judgment. Some personal property, including valuable things like motor vehicles and new property (retirement benefits, businesses, etc.) must also be divided individually. But you can divide most personal property, such as household goods, clothing, and personal items, by just splitting it up. "Property Division Provisions" in Appendix F has more information and sample provisions for all kinds of property divisions.

Does My Property Need Protection?

Divorce sometimes puts property at risk. Spouses may try to transfer property to others, before or during the divorce, to keep it out of the property division. If the divorce is bitter, spouses may take out their frustrations on the property. A while ago, a Macomb County woman got back at her husband by destroying his collection of rare Frank Sinatra records (when Sinatra read about the incident he graciously offered to replace some of the discs). But that's nothing compared to a Seattle husband who, to spite his wife, took a bulldozer and demolished their $90,000 house!

Michigan courts have the power to prevent this kind of mischief. They can issue orders protecting property from transfer or destruction. Regrettably, this book doesn't have the instructions and forms to get these orders, so see a lawyer if you need one.

Debts can also jeopardize property and wealth during divorce. Financial stability often breaks down amid a divorce, as spouses are tempted to run up debts on joint accounts. Both spouses are liable for these joint debts regardless of which spouse incurred them. Thus, it's a good idea to close or at least freeze all joint accounts (credit card, charge accounts, etc.), if possible, immediately after separation.

You can close a joint account quickly if no debts remain in the account. If debts exist, you can pay these off or sometimes transfer them to individual accounts. Another option is to freeze the account, so no new debt is added, followed by payment later.

Do I Need to Change My Estate Plan?

Married couples often have estate plans mirroring each other. The husband's will may give all his property to the wife, and name her as personal representative, with her will doing the same. Or they may have living (*inter vivos*) trusts with each other as trustee and beneficiary. Their financial and health care powers of attorney may appoint the other spouse as agent. Spouses may also be the beneficiaries of life insurance and retirement benefits.

Even without an estate plan, spouses are entitled, by law, to many estate rights. These include the right to a share of a spouse's estate, dower (an estate that widows have in their husbands' real property) and other allowances from the spouse's estate.

As explained in "After Your Divorce" on page 97, a divorce terminates all these estate rights. But there is always a risk that one spouse may die or become incapacitated *during* the divorce, giving the other control of the property. If you're in good health, this risk is small and probably not worth worrying about. But if you're in poor health, you may want to do some quick estate planning during the divorce.

There are a few things you can do yourself without a lawyer. You can revise your will or living trust naming a new personal representative in the will or a new trustee/beneficiaries in the trust. If you've appointed your spouse as agent under a financial or health care power of attorney, you can make a new one with another agent. And unless you and your spouse have agreed otherwise, you can change the designation of your spouse as beneficiary of your life insurance and retirement benefits.

To do more, you're going to need legal help. In Michigan, you normally cannot totally disinherit your spouse by will, since spouses are guaranteed a minimum share of the estate. However, a lawyer can prepare a will for you reducing your spouse's share to that legal minimum. In exceptional cases, spouses can lose their estate rights by marital misconduct (bigamy, absence, desertion, neglect for one year or more). A lawyer can tell you whether you qualify for this exception, and how to disinherit your spouse if you do.

A lawyer can also advise you about releasing estate rights. You may have already done that in a prenuptial agreement. The lawyer can tell you whether the release was effective. It's also possible to release estate rights in a postnuptial agreement (signed after marriage), especially during a separation leading to divorce. A lawyer should prepare that kind of agreement. After any release of estate rights, you are free to benefit whomever you like in your will.

With a lawyer's help, you could also convert any joint tenancy property (also known as tenancy by the entirety property) into tenancy in common ownership. Unlike other forms of property, tenancy in common doesn't have rights of survivorship. So when a spouse-owner dies, the surviving spouse doesn't get everything. Instead, the deceased spouse's estate and the surviving spouse split the property. This division makes tenancy in common ideal for estranged spouses who want to keep their shares of joint property separate.

Do I Need "Preliminary Relief"?

In most lawsuits, you normally don't get any relief (the things you're asking for in your lawsuit) unless and until you win the case. But in divorce cases it's possible to get some relief before the end of the divorce.

As mentioned in "Alimony" on page 11, courts may decide alimony on a temporary basis. And as pointed out previously in this part, courts can do some emergency property division/protection during divorces. If a court grants such preliminary relief, the issue is decided until the end of the case when the court makes a final decision in the divorce judgment.

Preliminary relief is important in contested cases, both for practical and tactical reasons. But the relief can be useful in uncontested ones as well. The trouble is, the legal procedures for getting preliminary relief are complicated, so this book doesn't have instructions or forms for this type of relief.

As useful as preliminary relief is, it isn't required in divorce cases, and you can often get by without it. When you are self-sufficient, you may not need any preliminary alimony or property. Or if the defendant is unavailable or unable to provide any support, it may not even be worth seeking.

If you believe preliminary relief is necessary, you may be able to improvise a substitute. You and the defendant can arrange to have the equivalent of preliminary relief provided privately out of court. For example, you both could divide property informally and/or have alimony paid without a court order, while your divorce is pending. This arrangement would resemble what you might obtain in preliminary relief from the court, except that it wouldn't be legally enforceable.*

If this substitute won't work, and you believe you must have preliminary relief, see a lawyer. The lawyer can prepare the necessary papers to seek the relief from the court.

Can I Socialize during the Divorce?

> ### More Information
>
> On adjusting to life during and after divorce:
>
> *Creative Divorce*, Mel Krantzler, New York: M. Evans and Company, Inc., 1973
>
> *The Good Divorce*, Constance Ahrons, New York: Harper-Collins, 1994

As couples split up, they often wonder whether they can start new social or sexual relationships. What you do during separation and divorce ought to be your own business. But regrettably, extramarital activity can be interpreted as marital fault, which could hurt you.

In a contested divorce, marital fault from extramarital activity may influence property division and alimony. Marital fault usually doesn't cause problems in uncontested cases as long as everything remains agreeable. But the fault can become an issue if your agreement over the divorce falls apart.

As a result, use your common sense as you begin your single life. You don't have to live like a hermit. But you should be discreet in your new social and sexual relationships. That will prevent any possible legal trouble.

Can I Keep the Divorce Secret?

Although court files are public records, courts have the power to restrict access to the contents of files by sealing them. In fact, courts once routinely sealed divorce cases between wealthy or influential people.

---

* Another problem with paying alimony informally out of court is that the payer won't be entitled to an income tax deduction for the payments, since they're not being paid in a divorce document.

In 1991, new court rules were adopted governing court secrecy. Now one must file a motion to seal a file and convince the court that there is "good cause" for sealing.* Because of these rules, it's difficult to have divorce files sealed. If you want to try to get your file sealed, contact a lawyer for help.

Some local newspapers cover legal news and publish lists of divorces granted by the courts in their area. There is really no way to keep that information out of the papers, since the completion of a divorce is a matter of public record even if the divorce file itself has been sealed.

Will I Have Tax Problems from the Divorce?

At one time, divorce was a tax nightmare. Not only were the tax rules for divorce complex, divorce itself had many negative tax consequences. These rules were changed by the Tax Reform Act of 1984 (TRA). The TRA is a rare example of a tax law that actually made the law simpler and fairer.

The TRA defined which divorce-related payments qualify as alimony (see "Alimony" on page 11 for more about these alimony tax rules). But the TRA didn't alter how alimony is taxed. It's still income for the recipient and a deduction (technically an adjustment to gross income) for the payer.

The most far-reaching change wrought by the TRA was to make all transfers of property between divorcing spouses non-taxable. Previously, spouses could gain or lose income from the property divisions of their divorces. Such gain or loss from a divorce is no longer possible under the new law, although income tax problems can still crop up later when a spouse sells property obtained in the divorce.

> ## More Information
>
> On taxes and divorce, obtain "Tax Information for Divorced or Separated Individuals" (Pub. 504), which is available from an IRS office, by calling the agency at (800) 829-3676, or you can view the document on the IRS Web site at www.irs.gov.

What If My Spouse Is Mentally Incompetent?

If your spouse has been declared mentally incompetent by a probate court, s/he must be specially represented in the divorce. After a declaration of mental incompetency, the probate court may appoint a conservator (a representative like a guardian) to manage the incompetent's affairs. A conservator has the authority to represent the incompetent in a divorce.

If you have been appointed as your spouse's conservator, you won't be able to represent him/her in the divorce because of the obvious conflict of interest. But you can ask the probate court for appointment of another person as conservator, and the new conservator could handle the divorce.

---

* A related problem is editing papers, which the defendant must receive, to keep selected personal information out of the hands of a defendant-spouse abuser. See "Keeping Personal Information away from a Spouse-Abuser" on page 42 for more about this issue.

An alternative is to have a *guardian ad litem* (GAL) appointed for your mentally incompetent spouse. While a conservator has broad powers to manage affairs, a GAL's authority is limited to representing the incompetent in a single lawsuit. In a divorce, the court handling the divorce, not a probate court, can appoint a GAL for a spouse after the divorce is filed.

Whatever arrangements are made for your incompetent spouse, they should be completed before or soon after you file your divorce. Then you can serve the spouse's conservator or GAL with the divorce papers, and the divorce can proceed normally.

What If I Need to File for Bankruptcy?

Divorce and bankruptcy seem to go together because financial problems often cause divorce. According to one study, divorced people file for bankruptcy at three times the rate of the nondivorced population. Despite this link, divorce and bankruptcy aren't as compatible as they ought to be. Each procedure requires a separate case, filed in different court systems (divorce in state court; bankruptcy in federal court), using different laws and rules.

Because of these problems, if you're considering both a divorce and a bankruptcy, seek legal advice. The lawyer can advise you about the relationship between divorce and bankruptcy, which type of bankruptcy to file (there are several), and whether to file singly or jointly (even separated spouses are permitted to file joint bankruptcies).

Don't wait to get legal help, because the timing of a divorce and bankruptcy can be important. In some cases, it's better to file the bankruptcy before completion of the divorce to protect exempt marital property. In other cases, the divorce should be finished before the bankruptcy is started so that some debts and obligations—but never alimony—can be wiped out. There are no firm rules about the sequence of cases; the timing will depend on the nature of your property and debts. Your lawyer should be able to explain what's best in your situation.

What If I Want to Dismiss the Divorce?

According to one estimate, 20-30% of all divorces are voluntarily withdrawn and dismissed. No one knows the exact reason for all these dismissals, but it's reasonable to assume that most cases were dropped after the spouses reconciled.

There's no penalty for withdrawing your divorce after you start it. On the contrary, Michigan law encourages reconciliation and dismissal at every step of a divorce. That's what the statutory waiting period is for. If you and your spouse decide to reconcile, see Appendix E for instructions and the form to dismiss your divorce.

What If My Spouse Abuses Me?

The physical abuse of one spouse by the other—usually, but not always, a wife at the hands of her husband—has been a constant problem with marriage and divorce. It's been estimated that spouse abuse is a problem in one out of three marriages. Sometimes this domestic violence becomes deadly. According to recent FBI figures, nearly a third of all female homicide victims are murdered by either their husbands or boyfriends.

For years, the legal system offered abused spouses little protection. It often seemed that family violence was a private matter into which the legal system wouldn't intervene. But that attitude has changed, and Michigan's spouse abuse laws have been toughened recently. Today it's possible to get personal protection orders (PPOs) preventing your spouse from:

- assaulting, attacking, beating, wounding or molesting you or someone else
- threatening to kill or physically injure you or someone else
- any act or conduct interfering with personal liberty or causing a reasonable apprehension of violence, such as stalking, harassment or unwanted contact
- interfering with you at work or school
- having access to your personal records or those of your children to get information about you
- purchasing or possessing a firearm
- entering property (so that your spouse can be ordered away from your home, even when it's the joint marital home)
- interfering with your removal of personal property or children from your spouse's property
- removing minor children from the person with legal custody, except as allowed by a court order

> ## More Information
>
> About spouse abuse, get:
>
> *Getting Free: You Can End Abuse and Take Back Your Life*, Ginny Nicarthy, Seattle: The Seal Press, 1997
>
> On Michigan's spouse abuse laws, ask your state senator or representative for a *Survivor's Handbook for Battered Women*.
>
> Call the **National Spouse Abuse Hotline** at (800) 799-7233 for referral to a spouse abuse shelter in your area.

You don't have to wait until a divorce to get a PPO. They're available anytime there's domestic abuse, even before you file. After filing, you can get a PPO while the divorce is pending. It's also possible to get a permanent PPO in your divorce judgment, which can remain in effect for any specified period of time.

When a spouse violates a PPO, s/he can be immediately arrested by the police, even if they didn't see the offense. Violation of a PPO is both a civil and criminal contempt of court, punishable by a maximum fine of $500 and 93 days in jail.

For all the protection it offers, Michigan's PPO law is complicated, making it difficult for nonlawyers to use. That's why it's best to have a lawyer when you're facing spouse abuse. If you have a low income, contact legal aid. The legal aid offices are very busy, but they usually give priority to spouse abuse cases. Or you can rely on a private lawyer for help. If you're determined to represent yourself, you can obtain PPO forms and instructions from the clerk of your circuit or family court. Since 1994, all Michigan circuit and family courts must make these materials available.

Whatever you do, keep in mind that a PPO cannot guarantee your safety. A court order is only a piece of paper; it won't stop someone bent on violence. If you believe your spouse is determined to harm you, take whatever precautions are necessary to protect yourself—with or without a PPO. This may even mean moving to a safe place. You may be able to find refuge with a friend or relative. There are also special shelters for abused spouses (and their children). Michigan has around 50 shelters serving every part of the state.

Keeping Personal Information away from a Spouse-Abuser

Several divorce papers contain personal information about you, where you live and sometimes your employment. During the divorce, the defendant gets copies of these papers.

If there's a danger of spouse abuse from the defendant, and you're keeping a distance, you may not want to reveal your current address and employment to the defendant. In exceptional cases like this, you can receive permission to withhold personal information from the divorce papers, and provide it separately and confidentially to the court. Ask the clerk about withholding personal information this way.

Where Can I File If My Spouse or I Am Native American?

Did you know that Michigan has the largest Native American population in the Eastern United States? Michigan has 12 federally-recognized Indian tribes and 4 which are recognized by the state. These tribes keep tribal rolls listing all members of the tribe (persons not on these rolls aren't regarded as members). The tribes often have their own reservations with separate tribal court systems which can grant divorces.

Native Americans can always file for divorce in regular state courts. But if they live in "Indian country" (reservation land plus satellite communities), they may have the option of filing in a tribal court. A divorce they receive there will be according to tribal law, which can be very different from the law described in this book.

> **More Information**
>
> About divorce in tribal courts, contact:
>
> **Michigan Indian Legal Services**
> 814 S. Garfield Ave.
> Suite A
> Traverse City, MI 49686
> (800) 968-6877

What If My Spouse or I Am an "Alien" (Noncitizen)?

If you or your spouse are aliens, your foreign nationality probably won't prevent you from getting a divorce in Michigan (see below about aliens and jurisdiction). But your alien status can have all kinds of hidden effects on the divorce, which are also explained below.

Can an Alien Get a Divorce in Michigan?

In the United States, divorce jurisdiction is based on residence. If you reside here you can get a divorce, regardless of your nationality. But in other countries, particularly civil law areas (basically the non-English speaking world), divorce jurisdiction is usually determined by nationality, not residence. In these countries, you must be a citizen to get a divorce. A few countries, such as Ireland, don't bother with divorce jurisdiction at all because they refuse to permit divorce.

If you're a citizen of one of those countries, a divorce you get in Michigan might not be recognized in your country. This won't be a problem if you have broken all ties with the country. But it could spell trouble if you intend to return to the country, or have children or property there. To find out how a Michigan divorce will be treated in your native country, check with your embassy or consulate.

Divorce by a Plaintiff-Alien

An alien living in Michigan can usually file for divorce here, and the divorce will go through. What an alien must consider is the impact the divorce will have on his/her residence rights. The impact is different for two types of aliens:

Immigrant. Aliens married to U.S. citizens typically apply for permanent residence here as spouses of citizens, becoming "lawful permanent residents." Aliens married two years or more quickly gain permanent residence. But aliens in shorter marriages usually get conditional residence, because of a suspicion that the marriage might be a sham.

A divorce during the two-year conditional residence period can be a problem for an immigrant. The divorce itself doesn't prove that the marriage is a sham (that's judged by the parties' intentions when they got married). But a divorce makes it more difficult to prove the marriage is real, especially without the help of an estranged spouse.

Nonimmigrant. A divorce can jeopardize the residence rights of a nonimmigrant, particularly if admission status depends solely on marriage. After the marriage is terminated by the divorce, this status is gone and the nonimmigrant may face deportation (there are some exceptions if there has been spouse/child abuse or in cases of extreme hardship).

> ## Glossary
>
> *Immigrant*—an alien who intends to settle in the country permanently.
>
> *Nonimmigrant*—an alien who is staying in the country temporarily.

Plaintiff-Citizen Filing against a Defendant-Alien

As a U.S. citizen filing for divorce, your citizenship is secure, and won't be affected by the divorce. The divorce could have an impact on the defendant-alien's residence rights, as described above. Nevertheless, the divorce could have an unforeseen effect on you.

Typically, U.S. citizens marrying aliens seek residence rights for them by filing a support affidavit. The affidavit promises to support the alien-spouse or else reimburse the government for any public assistance the alien might receive until the alien: 1) becomes a U.S. citizen 2) establishes an earnings record in the U.S. This obligation to support, which is actually a contract, survives divorce. So if you divorce an alien, and the alien receives public assistance, you could be liable for reimbursement.

Do You Need Legal Help?

If your divorce looks too complicated for you to do yourself, you need legal help. How do you find a good lawyer? The best way is by recommendation from someone you trust. But if you can't find a lawyer by word of mouth, legal services and referrals are available from:

Legal aid. Those who meet federal poverty guidelines are eligible for legal aid from one of the legal aid organizations located throughout the state. The problem is, these programs are often so understaffed that they can help only a fraction of those eligible for their services. To find the legal aid office in your area, look under "Attorneys" or "Social Service Organizations" in the yellow pages.

Legal clinics and services. Newspapers often carry advertisements for low-cost uncontested divorce services. Some of these services are offered by local attorneys doing business as clinics, while others may be branches of national legal service companies.

Lawyers. These days lawyers aren't shy about advertising, and you can find their ads in newspapers and the yellow pages. County bar associations in several of the larger counties provide lawyer referral services. To obtain lawyer referrals in other counties, call the state bar referral service at (800) 292-7850.

On the other hand, you may have decided that your divorce isn't too complicated. If that's true, you're ready to move on to Chapter 2 and begin your divorce.

Chapter 2

Legal Basics

Overview of Divorce Procedure

Doing Your Divorce

After Your Divorce

Legal Basics

For lawyers, an uncontested divorce isn't much more than a clerical task, which they usually assign to their secretaries. But nonlawyers are often stumped by the simplest things: How do I fill out the divorce papers? Where do I file them? When do I file them? How do I find the right court? This section deals with these legal basics and more, so you will be as well-prepared as any lawyer.

Court System

Before 1998, divorce cases were handled by the general circuit courts of Michigan. On January 1, 1998, Michigan's court system was reorganized and new family courts (which are technically divisions of the circuit courts) went into operation. Michigan family courts deal with all kinds of family-related cases: divorce (including post-divorce matters), annulment, separate maintenance, family support, custody, parenting time, paternity, domestic violence, child abuse and neglect, juvenile delinquency, guardianship/conservatorship, adoption, emancipation of minors and name change cases.

The philosophy of the family court system is to specialize in family law matters, unlike the general circuit courts which deal with all kinds of civil and criminal cases. Michigan family courts also have a "one-family, one-judge" policy, which brings all of a family's cases before the same judge, who is familiar with the family and its problems.

Family courts may be fairly new, but the court personnel haven't changed. The following people have responsibility for your divorce case:

Judge. Your divorce is handled by a family court judge, who is either a circuit court or probate court judge on assignment to the family court. You cannot choose the judge for your case. Ordinarily, when you file the clerk randomly assigns a judge to your case. But if you or members of your family have other family law cases pending in the court, the clerk will try to assign your divorce to the judge hearing the other case(s). With this assignment, the same judge will handle all the family's cases. If you dislike the judge, you cannot get another unless you can prove that the judge is actually biased or prejudiced against you.

Clerk. The family court clerk receives all your divorce papers and maintains a case file for them. Throughout this book, the family court clerk is simply called the clerk. In most counties, the county clerk is the clerk of the family court. But some counties have a special family court clerk, separate from the county clerk.

To find out who does the family court clerking in your county, call the county clerk and ask for information. Or simply look up the county government listing in the telephone book, and see if there is a separate listing for a clerk of the family division of the circuit court.

Courtroom clerk. The courtroom clerk sits in the courtroom next to the judge while the court is in session. During a trial, the courtroom clerk is responsible for marking and receiving exhibits. In an uncontested divorce case, the courtroom clerk has a smaller role, but in some counties s/he may receive and file papers during the final hearing.

Assignment clerk. Several larger counties use special assignment clerks to schedule court hearings. In these counties, final hearings in uncontested divorce cases may be scheduled through the assignment clerk.

Court reporter. The court reporter sits below the judge and records the court proceedings. In an uncontested divorce case, the court reporter makes a record of the final hearing, although it's unlikely that a transcript of the hearing will ever be needed.

Judge's secretary. Working in the judge's office, the judge's secretary may help in submitting papers to the judge for review.

Law clerk. Most judges have law clerks, who are often law students or new lawyers. Law clerks help judges with a number of tasks, including review of papers.

In many counties, these court personnel are conveniently located under one roof, usually in a courthouse or county building. But in other counties, whose court systems have outgrown their courthouses, court personnel may be scattered among several buildings. Before you begin your divorce, make sure you know where the court personnel are located.

The first person you want to find is the clerk, because you will begin your divorce in the clerk's office by filing the initial divorce papers there.

Papers

Many divorce-filers are surprised to find that courts won't do the divorce paperwork for you. Instead, it's your responsibility to prepare all the divorce papers. Don't try to do this all at once; prepare the papers as you need them, during each step of your divorce.

Preparing Papers

Whenever possible, type the divorce papers. But if you can't, it's permissible to print them by hand in ink. Either way, make sure the papers are neat and legible.

The divorce papers you file must also be accurate and honest. Judges can penalize those who intentionally or even carelessly file false legal papers. Ordinarily, these penalties are payments of money to opponents hurt by the false papers.

But for some false papers the penalties are severe. When you sign an affidavit, you swear to the notary public that the contents are true. You do much the same when you sign papers with a verification declaration ("I declare that the statements above are true to the best of my information, knowledge, and belief"). According to Michigan law, it's a crime to knowingly file a false affidavit, while the intentional falsification of a verified document is a contempt of court. Don't be alarmed by these penalties; just make sure that your papers are accurate and honest.

Among your divorce papers are several forms issued by the State Court Administrative Office (SCAO). These state forms include Michigan court forms and friend of the court forms, which are coded in the lower left corner by type (MC or FOC), number and date of release. Besides these state forms, a few counties, notably Wayne (number-coded), have local forms.

Added to the state forms are several Grand River Press forms (code: GRP/number/date). The Grand River Press forms include most of the

> ### More Information
>
> An affidavit is a legal paper stating facts that must be sworn to under oath before someone, such as a notary public, who can give oaths.
>
> To obtain notary services, look in the yellow pages under "Notaries Public," or contact insurance agencies, banks or mailing/shipping stores, which often have notary services available.

important divorce papers, such as the complaint, default and judgment. The state used to publish these forms, but discontinued publication in 1989. The Grand River Press forms have been created to replace them.

You may notice a difference in the type-size of the papers. On Jan. 1, 2004, a new court rule went into effect requiring that all court papers, except the state-issued (SCAO) forms, must be in 12-point type. Thus, the printing on all the GRP forms was increased to 12-point size. Also, when you fill in the papers, try to print or type in a larger size (no fine print) matching the printing on these forms.

The new court rule also specifies that all court papers must be 8½ x 11." Previously, this was the maximum size, but papers could be a little smaller. Prior editions of this book were 8½ x 11," making the perforated forms .25" smaller after detachment from the book (perforation of the forms causes a .25" loss in the binding margin). Now, the book has been increased in overall width by .25" to make up this difference.

Caption of Papers

Every form has a special purpose and each is prepared differently. Yet all the forms share similar captions which are filled in as follows:

STATE OF MICHIGAN Circuit Court - Family Division OJIBWAY COUNTY	JUDGMENT OF DIVORCE Page 1 of _____ pages	CASE NO. 89-00501—DO JUDGE TUBBS
Plaintiff (appearing *in propria persona*):		**Defendant:**
DARLENE ANN LOVELACE 121 S. MAIN LAKE CITY, MI 48800 772-0000	V	DUDLEY ERNEST LOVELACE 900 S. MAPLE LAKE CITY, MI 48800 773-3004

STATE OF MICHIGAN Circuit Court - Family Division OJIBWAY COUNTY	JUDGMENT OF DIVORCE Page 2 of _____ pages	CASE NO. 89-00501—DO
Plaintiff:		**Defendant:**
DARLENE ANN LOVELACE	V	DUDLEY ERNEST LOVELACE

As you can see, the papers have either a long or short caption. In a long caption, you must put the county where the divorce is filed in the upper left corner. The names, addresses and telephone numbers of you, as plaintiff, and your spouse, as defendant, go in the two large boxes. Some state-issued forms may ask for court or friend of the court addresses and telephone numbers. You can get this extra information from a telephone directory (look under the "County Government" listing in the blue (government) pages).

Incidentally, the italicized Latin phrase in the caption of many of the forms signals that this is a self-help divorce. *In propria persona* (sometimes abbreviated to *in pro per*) means "in your own person," indicating that you are doing the case yourself without a lawyer. Some of the state-issued forms, such as the Summons and Complaint (MC 01), have caption boxes for lawyer representatives. You can leave these boxes blank, or insert in them: "In Pro Per."

Your case number goes in the upper right corner. This number starts with a two-digit number for the year followed by several other numbers. It ends with a two-letter case-type code. All cases in Michigan have codes according to their type: A divorce with minor children bears a DM code and divorces without minor children have a DO code. Because a case number isn't assigned until filing, you won't have it for your initial divorce papers, so leave the case number spaces blank on them. But include your case number in the captions of all your other papers.

If you're in a larger county that has more than one family court judge, write the name of your judge below the case numbers on all the papers you file after the initial divorce papers. This will help direct the papers to the correct case file and judge.

With a short caption, you can omit much of the above information. All you need for a short caption is the court, case number, and your and your spouse's names as plaintiff and defendant.

Wayne County, which has the state's largest court system, has a caption-labeling system to prevent mishandling of court papers. When you file a divorce in Wayne County, the clerk prints strips of caption labels for both parties. Notice how the clerk takes several labels and affixes these to the captions of your initial divorce papers. As you file other papers, use labels from your strip to label them in the same way. Save the other strip of caption labels because you must have it served on the defendant later.

To Obtain

Extra copies of Wayne County forms, call the Wayne County Friend of the Court's form fax line at (313) 967-3662. The line has a menu where you can select the form you want, which is then faxed to a fax number you specify.

The Wayne County circuit court system also has a Web site, www.3rdcc.org, from which you can view and/or download forms.

You should have enough caption labels for all your papers. But if you run out, you can get more in the clerk's office in room 201 of the Coleman A. Young Municipal Center (CAYMC) (formerly the City-County Bldg.) at 2 Woodward Ave. in Detroit.

Copying Papers

As you prepare divorce papers, you must make several photocopies. Except for the Summons and Complaint (MC 01), make two photocopies of each divorce paper. This gives you enough divorce papers and copies to distribute as follows:

- original - court (clerk)
- 1st copy - plaintiff
- 2nd copy - defendant

When you photocopy divorce papers, copy both sides of any two-sided forms because some papers have important information on the reverse. Most two-sided forms are tumble-printed, with their reverse sides upside down. This makes it possible to read the reverse sides while the papers are fastened to a file folder by simply lifting them up. When you photocopy these two-sided forms, you might not be able to run your copies through the photocopier again to make a tumble-printed form. If so, just make the paper into a two-page form and staple the pages together.

With all these papers and copies, it's easy to get disorganized. To keep track of everything, prepare a file for all your divorce papers. Not only will this file keep you organized during the divorce, it will give you a complete record of the case afterward.

Filing Papers

When you file your divorce, the clerk will open a case file for your case. As you file papers, the clerk will ordinarily use the following procedure:

- keep the original for your case file
- return a true copy* for the plaintiff
- return a true copy for the defendant

You can file papers with the clerk personally, by mail or sometimes even by facsimile (fax). Despite these options, it's usually best to file the initial divorce papers in person and the other papers this way whenever you can. By filing personally, you can pay any fees that are due and immediately get back copies of your papers for service on the other party.

For filing by mail, send your papers and any fees to the clerk along with a cover letter asking for filing and return of the copies you have enclosed. To get copies back quickly, include a self-addressed envelope with postage.

Filing by fax isn't allowed when filing fees are due (unless you have paid in advance by depositing money with the clerk), because the clerk won't accept a filing without payment of the filing fee. Moreover, the clerk won't send or fax back copies of the papers you file, so there's no way to get copies. Thus, fax-filing should be used in emergency, when you have to file in a hurry to meet a filing deadline.

Fees

You must pay several fees to get a divorce (see "How Much Will My Divorce Cost?" on page 29 for a description of the fees). Except for the service fee,

---

*   When a clerk returns a copy of a paper to you, it may have a stamp or seal indicating that it's a true copy. This says that the copy is real. Try to get true copies of all papers you file, especially court orders such as the judgment.

you pay these fees to the clerk. Clerks usually accept cash, personal checks and money orders as payment. After you pay, the clerk may give you a receipt, which you should keep as proof of payment.

The service fee is paid outside of court. As mentioned before, you can choose from among several methods of service: 1) acknowledgment 2) mail 3) delivery. You can usually obtain service by acknowledgment for free. When you use service by mail, you pay the post office for the mailing. If you use service by delivery, you pay the server, who is usually a sheriff or commercial process server. Ordinarily, the server bills you for the service fee after service when s/he returns the proof of service to you. But if you use service by delivery out of town or out of state, it's a good idea to prepay the service fee. When you send the service papers to the server, include a check or money order for $30 or so, and a note asking the server to refund/bill you for the difference between your prepayment and his service fee.

If you qualify, you can get an exemption from payment of the court fees. You are exempt from payment if you are receiving public assistance or have a low income. Appendix A has more about qualifying for a fee exemption, and instructions and the affidavit to apply for the exemption.

If you've received a fee exemption, you won't have to pay any court fees during your divorce (although you might have to pay them at the end of the divorce). If the clerk tries to charge you a fee during your divorce, refer the clerk to the fee exemption affidavit, which will be in your case file.

> ## Courtroom Etiquette
>
> During a court hearing, you should follow these rules of courtroom behavior:
>
> - Dress neatly and be well-groomed.
> - Be on time.
> - Be courteous to the judge and others.
> - Wait until called on to speak.
> - Don't interrupt while the judge or others are talking; you will get your chance to speak.
> - After the judge makes a decision, don't persist in arguing your view.

Time

During your divorce, you must deal with several important time periods and deadlines, including: 1) 180-day state residence requirement 2) 10-day county residence requirement 3) answering period (usually 21 or 28 days) 4) statutory waiting period (60 days for divorces without minor children) 5) filing deadlines for various papers.

The court rules have detailed provisions to figure periods of time. For a time period of days, the period begins on the day after the day of an act (filing, service, establishment of residence, etc.); the day of the act itself isn't counted. The last day of the period is counted, unless it falls on a Saturday, Sunday or legal holiday. In that case, the period extends to the next day that isn't a Saturday, Sunday or legal holiday.

Example: You serve a defendant by mail on May 1. The 28-day answering period after service by mail begins on May 2 (the day after the day of service) and ends on May 29 (which in this example is not a Saturday, Sunday or legal holiday). The defendant has until May 29 to answer.

Example: You serve a defendant by mail on May 1. The 28-day answering period after service by mail begins on May 2 (the day after the day of service) and ends on May 29. But this year May 29 is Memorial Day, a legal holiday, so the answering period extends to May 30. The defendant must answer by May 30.

To avoid time problems, you can simply estimate the time period and then add a little more time for safety. For example, if you figure that a time period ends sometime during the first week of a month, you could wait until the middle of the month to take action, avoiding any danger of acting too quickly.

Courthouse Appearances

During your divorce, you must appear once in court before the judge. You may also have to make an informal appearance at the courthouse, outside the courtroom.

Court Hearings

All divorce plaintiffs are expected to attend a final hearing, in court before the judge, at the end of the case. During the hearing, you must give some brief testimony to get a Judgment of Divorce (GRP 4).

For a formal court hearing, make sure you know the location of the hearing beforehand. Court hearings normally take place in the courtroom of the judge assigned to your case, which is usually in the county courthouse or similar county building.

Go to the place of the court hearing on the scheduled day and time. Try to arrive around 30 minutes before the hearing, to take care of any last-minute business. By arriving early, you can also observe other hearings. Be prepared to spend most of the morning or afternoon at the hearing, since it may not start on time.

When your case is called by the courtroom clerk, step forward and identify yourself. Mention that you are representing yourself. Take a seat at one of the tables inside the bar (the gate) of the court, and get ready to begin your presentation.

Other Courthouse Appearances

The clerk may also ask you to attend a case conference, for scheduling or other reasons, outside of the courtroom. These are informal sessions held by court personnel without the judge. As with a formal court hearing, know where the meeting is held, be on time and observe normal courtroom etiquette.

Special Arrangements for a Courthouse Appearance

If you have a handicap (mobility, visual, speech or hearing impairment), court personnel can make special accommodations for your courthouse appearance. For non-English-speakers, the court can appoint an interpreter to translate the proceedings into your language.

Handicapper Accommodations

Tell court personnel about the handicap by preparing a Request for Accommodations (MC 70) (see the sample MC 70 at the end of this section). File or send the form to the clerk well ahead of the scheduled appearance. Court personnel will contact you before the appearance, and discuss the accommodation you need.

In exceptional cases, special accommodations aren't enough and you may be excused from the court appearance. If so, you can give information, such as testimony for a final hearing, in written or electronic form (by telephone, for example). Persons with severe handicaps may qualify for this exception. Prisoners are also frequently excused from court attendance, and can give written or electronic testimony (see "What If My Spouse or I Am Imprisoned?" on page 27 for more about this procedure).

Foreign Language Interpreters

The court can appoint a foreign language interpreter if you can't speak English well enough to understand the court proceedings. Use the Motion and Order for Appointment of Foreign Language Interpreter (MC 81) (a sample MC 81 appears at the end of this section). The judge may skip a hearing on this motion, and simply sign the order.

You could file the MC 81 any time during the divorce. Whenever you file, send a copy of the motion to the defendant, even if s/he has defaulted, at his or her last known address.

Incidentally, there are special foreign language Summons and Complaint (MC 01) forms available in Arabic, Chinese, Hmong, Korean, Russian and Spanish. You can get these from the clerk, and use the special forms if your spouse speaks one of these languages, but isn't fluent in English.

Local Rules and Forms

For years, there were variations in divorce procedures among Michigan's 83 counties. In 1993, the state tried to standardize procedures by abolishing all local divorce rules and forms. But little by little, several counties, Wayne in particular, have been permitted to re-adopt local rules and forms.

Don't panic if you encounter some local practices that aren't described in this book. Ask the local authorities what the local practice is and adapt to it. Luckily, variations tend to be minor. They typically concern scheduling the final hearing.

New Laws, Rules, Forms and Fees

These days, divorce laws, rules, forms and fees change regularly. Congress and the Michigan Legislature are constantly passing new divorce laws. Added to this are the thousands of decisions courts issue each year, some of which affect divorce.

As a result of this activity, parts of this book may become outdated. To keep the book current, Grand River Press offers an update about recent changes in divorce law. See the order form in the front of this book for update information.

To Obtain

Laws, court rules and other legal information, visit a law library. Most county courthouses have law libraries which are open to the public. The divorce laws are in the MCLAs (Michigan Compiled Laws Annotated) and MSAs (Michigan Statutes Annotated); the court rules are published in *Michigan Rules of Court - State* by the West Group (this volume also includes all the local court rules).

Online, you can access Michigan law via www.michiganlegislature.org, using the search engine to search by section or subject. The basic divorce laws are MCL 552.1-552.1803.

For court rules, go to www.courts.michigan.gov/supremecourt, scroll down and click on the "Court Rules Online" icon, and a table of contents will pop up with several choices: 1) under "Michigan Court Rules," select "Chapter 3 Special Proceedings and Actions" for the divorce court rules of MCR 3.201-3.219. 2) under "Local Court Rules," select "Circuit Courts" for local court rules arranged by county.

Approved, SCAO

REQUEST FOR ACCOMMODATIONS

Court name and location
OJIBWAY COUNTY CIRCUIT COURT-FAMILY DIVISION
200 N. MAIN
LAKE CITY, MI 48800

Instructions for completing form: Provide your name, address, and telephone number. Check the boxes which apply to you and provide any necessary details. When you have completed this request, please return it to the court at the above address.

Today's date
8-10-89

1. Name
DARLENE A. LOVELACE

Address
121 S. MAIN

	State	Zip	Telephone no.
	MI	48800	772-0000

City
LAKE CITY

2. Court activity you need accommodations for:

☒ Hearing 9-7-89
_____ Date

☐ Mediation meeting _____ Date

☐ Jury duty _____ Date(s)

☐ Other (specify): _____ include dates if relevant

3. What is the nature of your disability?

☒ Physical mobility impairment (wheelchair, walker, crutches, etc.)

☐ Speech impairment (specify): _____

☐ Visual impairment

☐ Hearing impairment (specify)   ☐ deaf   ☐ hard of hearing

☐ Other (specify): _____

4. What type of accommodation are you requesting?

☐ Interpreter for deaf (specify whether ASL, tactile, oral, etc.) _____

☐ Assistive listening device (specify type of device) _____

☒ Physical location accessible for persons with a physical mobility concern.

☐ Other (specify) _____

For court use only

MC 70 (10/97) REQUEST FOR ACCOMMODATIONS

Approved, SCAO

Original - Court file
1st copy - Assignment Clerk/Extra
2nd copy - Friend of the Court/Extra

3rd copy - Opposing party
4th copy - Moving party

STATE OF MICHIGAN
JUDICIAL DISTRICT
JUDICIAL CIRCUIT
COUNTY

MOTION AND ORDER FOR APPOINTMENT
OF FOREIGN LANGUAGE INTERPRETER

CASE NO.

Court address

Court telephone no.

Plaintiff name(s)

☒ moving party

Plaintiff's attorney, bar no., address, and telephone no.

v

Defendant name(s)

☐ moving party

Defendant's attorney, bar no., address, and telephone no.

MOTION

1. I state that I am unable to speak English sufficiently to understand and participate in the proceedings in this case.
2. ☐ I am represented by an attorney.   ☒ I am not represented by an attorney.
3. I request the court to appoint a foreign language interpreter to interpret for me.
4. I request an interpreter who speaks the _KOREAN_ language.
5. If required, place my request on the motion calendar.

_4-1-89_
Date

Darlene A. Lovelace
Signature

To be completed only if the court
requires a hearing on the motion

NOTICE OF HEARING

You are notified that a hearing has been scheduled on this matter for:

Judge

Hearing location	Bar no.	Date	Time
☐ Court address above ☐			

If you require special accommodations to use the court because of disabilities, please contact the court immediately to make arrangements.

_____
Date

_____
Signature

CERTIFICATE OF MAILING

I certify that on this date I mailed a copy of this motion and notice of hearing (if applicable) to the other party at the last known address.

_4-1-89_
Date

Darlene A. Lovelace
Signature

IT IS ORDERED the above motion is

ORDER

_4-15-89_
Date

☒ granted.   ☐ denied.

Lester Jubbs
Judge

MC 81 (10/01) **MOTION AND ORDER FOR APPOINTMENT OF FOREIGN LANGUAGE INTERPRETER**

THE CLERK WILL SCHEDULE A HEARING ON THE MOTION, IF NECESSARY.

Overview of Divorce Procedure

At first, divorce procedure may seem forbidding. But it's really not so mysterious when you break it down into steps and understand the purpose of each step.

Like any lawsuit, a divorce starts when the plaintiff files a paper known as a complaint. Despite its rather alarming name, a complaint is simply the document that starts a lawsuit. A divorce complaint contains facts about the parties and their marriage, and then asks for relief on the divorce issues. At filing, the clerk issues a summons in the case notifying the defendant that a divorce has been filed. These papers (and possibly others) make up the initial divorce papers.

The defendant must get notice of the divorce by receiving the initial divorce papers. Notice is provided by serving these papers on the defendant. There are three regular methods of service, plus a couple of alternate service methods for elusive or disappeared defendants.

After service, the defendant may respond to the plaintiff's complaint within an answering period. The defendant's response can be either by filing: 1) an answer to the complaint or 2) a motion objecting to the complaint.

In the vast majority of cases, defendants don't bother to respond, putting them in default. The plaintiff can then go to the clerk and have the defendant's default declared. With this declaration, the case is officially an uncontested divorce, or what lawyers sometimes call a *pro confesso* or "pro con" divorce case.

But if the defendant responds to the complaint within the answering period, the divorce is contested. In that case, the plaintiff should seek a lawyer to take over the case because it's difficult to handle a contested case without a lawyer.

After the 60-day statutory waiting period, the plaintiff can get the Judgment of Divorce, which decides all the divorce issues, during the final hearing. The plaintiff must appear at the hearing and give testimony or "proofs" in support of the judgment. This sounds scary, but the final hearing is usually very brief and easy to get through. After the final hearing, the plaintiff files the divorce judgment making the divorce final.

This book has organized the divorce procedure into four steps: "Filing," "Service," "Default" and "Final Hearing." The flowchart below summarizes these steps and the time to perform them.

1 Filing

Preparing Your Initial Divorce Papers

You begin your divorce by preparing the initial divorce papers. These papers include the complaint and summons. The divorce complaint describes the basic facts of your marriage. It also tells the court that your marriage has broken down by citing the no-fault grounds for divorce. Finally, the complaint asks the court to decide the divorce issues. The purpose of the summons is to notify the defendant that you have filed a divorce complaint, and that s/he may respond to it.

The complaint and summons are contained in a set of forms: the Summons and Complaint (MC 01) and Complaint for Divorce (GRP 1). The Summons and Complaint (MC 01) includes the summons in the case along with the first part of the complaint. The Complaint for Divorce (GRP 1) is actually a continuation of this form and contains the main body of the complaint.

Optional and Local Forms

Your initial divorce papers will include the Affidavit and Order, Suspension of Fees/Costs (MC 20) when you want a fee exemption (see Appendix A for the form and instructions). You must file an extra paper and take other special steps if you seek alimony (see Appendix C for the details).

The blank forms for the initial divorce papers and all other divorce papers are located in the forms section in the back of this book. Optional forms like the Affidavit and Order, Suspension of Fees/Costs (MC 20), and local forms like the Certificate of Conformity for Domestic Relations Order or Judgment (1225) (filed at the end of Wayne County divorces) are located in a special section. All the forms are perforated so you can easily tear them out of the book.

There are filled-in samples of the initial divorce papers at the end of this section; other sample forms appear at the end of the sections they relate to by subject matter. For general information about form preparation, see "Papers" on page 49.

Ordinarily, you must make two photocopies of your divorce papers. The clerk gets the original, leaving copies for the defendant and you. But you will need an extra copy of the Summons and Complaint (MC 01), giving you the following papers:

● Summons and Complaint	MC 01	3
● Complaint for Divorce	GRP 1	2
★ Affidavit and Order, Suspension of Fees/Costs	MC 20	2

Filing Your Divorce

Start your divorce by filing it with the clerk (see "Court System" on page 47 for information about finding the clerk). To file, you must have your initial divorce papers ready. And unless you receive a fee exemption, you must pay the filing fee (see "How Much Will My Divorce Cost?" on page 29 for the amount of the filing fee). In all, you should have the following items when you go to the clerk's office to file your divorce:

● Summons and Complaint — MC 01
  ● original
  ● 3 copies

● Complaint for Divorce — GRP 1
  ● original
  ● 2 copies

● money for the filing fee

★ Affidavit and Order, Suspension of Fees/Costs — MC 20
  ● original
  ● 2 copies

When you arrive at the clerk's office, tell the clerk that you want to file a divorce complaint. The clerk should then do the following to file your divorce:

- Take the Summons and Complaint (MC 01) and the three copies and: 1) assign a judge to the case and stamp his/her name on these papers 2) enter a case number on them 3) complete the summons boxes in the middle of the papers. File the Summons and Complaint (MC 01) and return three copies to you.

- File the Complaint for Divorce (GRP 1) and return two copies to you.

- Take the money for the filing fee

★ File the Affidavit and Order, Suspension of Fees/Costs (MC 20), if used, to suspend the fees immediately; or submit the form to the judge for consideration, and then return two copies to you.

✦ In Wayne County only, prepare caption labels, label the captions of the initial divorce papers and give you two strips of caption labels.

To Obtain

If the clerk doesn't have Record of Divorce or Annulment (DCH-0838) forms, these are also available from:

Department of Community Health
Division for Vital Records and Health Studies
P.O. Box 30195
Lansing, MI 48909
(517) 335-8496

Before you leave the clerk's office, ask for a Record of Divorce or Annulment (DCH-0838). This form asks for personal and marital information. You complete and file it at the end of the divorce, when you get the judgment. After filing, the clerk sends the DCH-0838 to the Michigan Department of Community Health for addition to the state's vital records. Although you won't use the form until later, it's convenient to pick it up now while you're at the clerk's office.

STATE OF MICHIGAN

Approved, SCAO

Original - Court
1st copy - Defendant

2nd copy - Plaintiff
3rd copy - Return

CASE NO.

JUDICIAL DISTRICT
JUDICIAL CIRCUIT
COUNTY PROBATE

SUMMONS AND COMPLAINT

Court tele

FILL OUT CAPTION
ON THIS AND ALL
OTHER PAPERS
AS SHOWN
IN "PREPARING
PAPERS"

Court address

Plaintiff name(s), address(es), and telephone no(s)

v

Defendant name(s), address(es), and telephone no(s).

Plaintiff attorney, bar no., address, and telephone no.

CLERK WILL
COMPLETE
SUMMONS BOXES

SUMMONS   NOTICE TO THE DEFENDANT: In the name of the people of the State of Michigan you are notified:
1. You are being sued.
2. YOU HAVE 21 DAYS after receiving this summons to file an answer with the court and serve a copy on the other party
   take other lawful action (28 days if you were served by mail or you were served outside this state).
3. If you do not answer or take other action within the time allowed, judgment may be entered against you for the relief dem
   in the complaint.

Issued	This summons expires	Court clerk
3-1-89	5-31-89	Martha Gee

*This summons is invalid unless served on or before its expiration date.

COMPLAINT   Instruction: The following is information that is required to be in the caption of every complaint and is to be completed
by the plaintiff. Actual allegations and the claim for relief must be stated on additional complaint pages and attached to this form.

Family Division Cases
☒ There is no other pending or resolved action within the jurisdiction of the family division of circuit court involving the family or family
  members of the parties.
☐ An action within the jurisdiction of the family division of the circuit court involving the family or family members of the parties
  has been previously filed in _____ Court.

The action ☐ remains ☐ is no longer pending. The docket number and the judge assigned to the action a

Docket no.	Judge

DESCRIBE ANY
PRIOR FAMILY CASES
INVOLVING YOU OR YOUR
FAMILY, SO DIVORCE CAN
BE DIRECTED TO FAMILY
COURT JUDGE HANDLING
PRIOR CASES

General Civil Cases
☒ There is no other pending or resolved civil action arising out of the same transaction or occurrence as alleged in
☐ A civil action between these parties or other parties arising out of the transaction or occurrence alleged in the
  been previously filed in _____ pending. The docket number and the judge assigned to the ac

The action ☐ remains ☐ is no longer pending. The docket number and the judge assigned to the ac

Docket no.	Judge

VENUE
Plaintiff(s) residence (include city, township, or village)   (SEE CAPTIONS ABOVE)

Defendant(s) residence (include city, township, or village)

Place where action arose or business conducted

Darlene A. Lovelace
Signature of attorney/plaintiff

2-28-89
Date

If you require special accommodations to use the court because of a disability or if you require a foreign language interpreter to help
you to fully participate in court proceedings, please contact the court immediately to make arrangements.

MC 01 (6/03) SUMMONS AND COMPLAINT   MCR 2.102(B)(11), MCR 2.104, MCR 2.105, MCR 2.107, MCR 2.113(C)(2)(a), (b), MCR 3.206(A)

2 Service

Due process requires that the defendant receive notice of the divorce so s/he can respond to it. Notice is provided by serving copies of the initial divorce papers on the defendant. You should begin service as soon as possible, within a few days after filing.

Although the purpose of service is notice, don't assume that you can skip it when the defendant already knows about the divorce. And don't try to serve the defendant by simply giving the divorce papers to him/her. No doubt your spouse would get informal notice of the divorce these ways. But the law requires that the defendant receive *official* notice of the divorce by service.

Official notice can only be accomplished by one of the service methods described below. With one of these methods, the court knows for sure that the defendant got notice of the divorce. For this reason, service is absolutely necessary. The service rules may seem artificial and even rather silly at times, but they must be followed carefully. If you omit service, or violate the service rules, there's a chance your whole divorce will be invalid.

There are three methods of serving defendants who are available to be served: 1) acknowledgment 2) mail 3) delivery. Each method can be used anywhere in the state of Michigan. These service methods can also be used outside the state (including foreign countries), as long as there is Michigan jurisdiction over the nonresident defendant (see "Can I Get a Divorce in Michigan?" on page 24 for more about jurisdiction).

Despite service's wide reach, there are a few minor restrictions on serving papers. The court rules disqualify you from serving the initial divorce papers personally because you're a party to the case. Instead, you must have a neutral third party serve the papers for you. If you use service by delivery, a professional server, such as a sheriff or commercial process server, can serve for you. But when you choose either service by acknowledgment or service by mail, you must enlist a helper (who can be any mentally competent adult), such as a friend, to help with service. The helper acts as a straw man through whose hands the divorce papers pass to the defendant.

Whichever service method you choose, you mustn't have the divorce papers served on a Sunday, an election day, or on the defendant while s/he is at, en route or returning from a court appearance. Michigan law gives people immunity from service in all these situations.

Preparing for Service

The defendant must be served with the papers listed below, which shall be referred to collectively as the "service papers:"

• Summons and Complaint   MC 01

• Complaint for Divorce   GRP 1

★ Affidavit and Order, Suspension of Fees/Costs   MC 20

✦ a strip of caption labels (in Wayne County only)

After the defendant is served with these papers, service must be proved in a proof of service. Each method of service (acknowledgment, mail, delivery) is proved differently. But all are proved in the Proof of Service on the reverse of your extra copy of the Summons and Complaint (MC 01). This paper will be referred to as the "proof of service copy of the Summons and Complaint (MC 01)." After service, you file it with the clerk so that your case file shows that the defendant was served.

Service by Acknowledgment

Service by acknowledgment is the simplest method of service. To use this method, you need the cooperation of the defendant and the assistance of a helper. If the defendant is in another county or state, you must find someone there to act as your helper.

Service is accomplished by having the helper hand the service papers to the defendant. You may be present during the transfer, but the helper, not you, must be the one who actually hands the service papers to the defendant. The day of service is the day the defendant receives the service papers from the helper.

Proving Service by Acknowledgment

Immediately after service, the helper should have the defendant date (with time and day) and sign the Acknowledgment of Service, which is at the bottom of the reverse of your proof of service copy of the Summons and Complaint (MC 01). Make two copies of this paper and save for filing later as your proof of service.

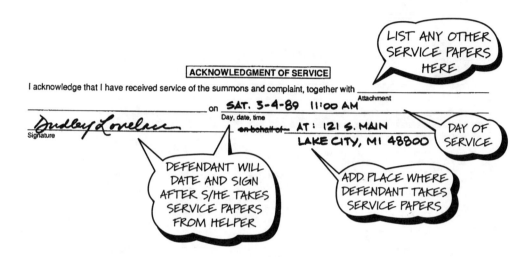

Service by Mail

Service by mail is a little more expensive than service by acknowledgment. But it's a very effective method of service because it goes anywhere U.S. mail is delivered—even overseas.* The court rules permit service by mail through either registered or certified mail. Because certified mail is cheaper than registered mail, certified mail is the best choice.

When you serve by mail, you need the assistance of a helper and the U.S. Postal Service. Your helper mails the service papers to the defendant and the postal service delivers these to him/her by certified mail.

To prove service, you need several special services available with certified mail: 1) restricted delivery 2) return receipt service. By restricting delivery, the service papers are delivered only to the defendant personally or someone s/he has designated in writing to receive mail. The return receipt

---

* The service by mail described above deals with mail sent inside the United States and to military mail overseas. For service by mail in foreign countries, ask the post office about recorded delivery, which is similar to domestic certified mail, and offers restricted delivery and return receipt services. The Recorded Delivery Receipt (PS Form 8099) explains this type of delivery.

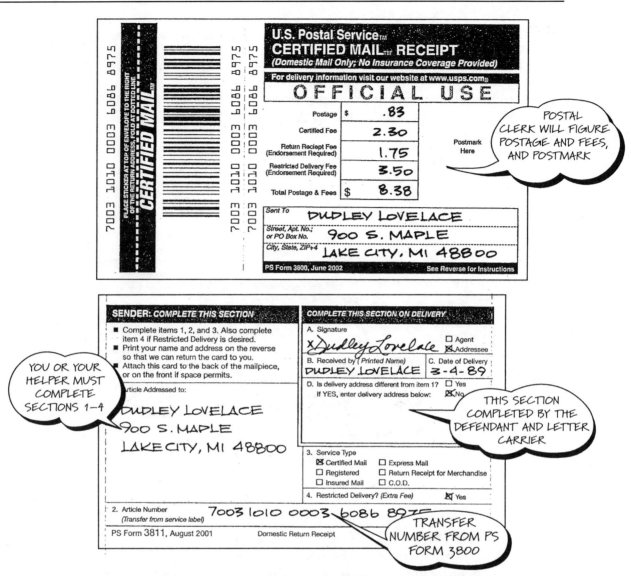

provides proof of who received the papers, the date of delivery and the address of delivery only if this is different from the address on the envelope. This receipt becomes a key part of the proof of service.

Before you have the service papers mailed, prepare the mailing by placing your service papers in an envelope addressed to the defendant with your helper's name and address as the return address. In addition, you or your helper must prepare two certified mail forms: 1) Certified Mail Receipt (PS Form 3800) 2) Domestic Return Receipt (PS Form 3811), which are available at any post office.

On the PS Form 3800, fill in the defendant's name and address at the bottom of the form. For the PS Form 3811, write your helper's name and address on the front of the card, and on the reverse complete boxes #1-4. In section #2, transfer the article number from the PS Form 3800. In section #3, check the certified mail box, and ask for restricted delivery in #4.

After you complete the PS Form 3800 and 3811, peel off the plastic strips on the ends of the PS 3811 and attach the card to the envelope (there probably won't be room on the front of the envelope, so attach it to the reverse side).

PROOF OF SERVICE	SUMMONS AND COMPLAINT Case No.

TO PROCESS SERVER: You are to serve the summons and complaint not later than 91 days from the date of filing or the date of expiration on the order for second summons. You must make and file your return with the court clerk. If you are unable to complete service you must return this original and all copies to the court clerk.

CERTIFICATE / AFFIDAVIT OF SERVICE / NON-SERVICE

☐ **OFFICER CERTIFICATE** OR ☒ **AFFIDAVIT OF PROCESS SERVER**

I certify that I am a sheriff, deputy sheriff, bailiff, appointed court officer, or attorney for a party [MCR 2.104(A)(2)], and that: (notarization not required)

Being first duly sworn, I state that I am a legally competent adult who is not a p... ...e party, and that: (notarizati...

LIST ANY OTHER SERVICE PAPERS HERE

☐ I served personally a copy of the summons and complaint,
☒ I served by registered or certified mail (copy of return receipt attached) a copy of t...

together with _____
List all documents served with the Summons and Complaint

_____ on the defendant(s):

Defendant's name	Complete address(es) of service	Day, date, time
DUDLEY LOVELACE	900 S. MAPLE, LAKE CITY, MI 48800	SAT. 3-4-89

GET DATE FROM PS FORM 3811 *DAY OF SERVICE*

☐ I have personally attempted to serve the summons and complaint, together with any attachments on the following defendant(s) and have been unable to complete service.

Defendant's name	Complete address(es) of service	Day, date, time

Service fee	Miles traveled	Mileage fee	Total fee
$		$	$

Signature *Ruth Darling*

Title

Subscribed and sworn to before me on **3-7-89**, **OJIBWAY** County, Michigan.
Date

My commission expires: **1-1-90** Signature: *Loretta Smiley*
Date Deputy court clerk/Notary public

On the front of the envelope, to the left of the defendant's address and below your helper's return address, write "Restricted Delivery" and "Return Receipt Requested" on the envelope. By making these notations (the PS Form 3800 calls this "endorsement"), you will remind the letter carrier to restrict delivery and get a receipt.

Have your helper take the envelope containing the service papers, with the Domestic Return Receipt (PS Form 3811) attached, the Certified Mail Receipt (PS Form 3800) and money to pay for the mailing to a post office window. The helper should ask the postal clerk to mail the envelope by certified mail with the special services you have written on the envelope. The clerk will prepare the certified mailing and return a postmarked for Certified Mail Receipt (PS Form 3800) to your helper. Keep this receipt for your records.

Later, a letter carrier will deliver the mailing to the defendant, get his/her name (printed), signature and other delivery information on the reverse of the Domestic Return Receipt (PS Form 3811). Within a few days, your helper should get the PS Form 3811 back in the mail. You can then have your helper prove the service as described below. The day of service is the day the defendant receives the mailing from the letter carrier.

If your helper gets the whole envelope back, instead of the Domestic Return Receipt (PS Form 3811) alone, service by mail has failed. The defendant may have refused to accept the mailing, wasn't home or has moved without leaving a current forwarding order. Whatever the case, you will have to abandon service by mail because it only works when the defendant is ready and willing to take the certified mailing from the letter carrier. If service by mail fails, try service by delivery instead.

Proving Service by Mail

After your helper gets the Domestic Return Receipt (PS Form 3811) back in the mail, have him/her prove service on the reverse of your proof of service copy of the Summons and Complaint (MC 01). Complete the information about the service by mail under the Affidavit of Process Server, and have the helper sign the form before a notary public. For guidance, see the sample proof of service by mail on the previous page.

As proof of the defendant's receipt of the mailing, staple the Domestic Return Receipt (PS Form 3811) to the reverse of your proof of service copy of the Summons and Complaint (MC 01). Make two copies of this paper and save one for filing later as your proof of service.

Service by Delivery

You can also obtain service by having someone deliver the service papers to the defendant. Any mentally competent adult except you can do that. If the defendant is cooperative, you could have a helper perform service by delivery for you. But in that case it would be much easier to have the defendant simply acknowledge delivery of the service papers from your helper and get service by acknowledgment. Therefore, it's likely that you will use service by delivery for defendants who live out of town or state, or are otherwise hard to serve.

Service by delivery is usually carried out by a professional server, such as a sheriff or commercial process server. Whatever other service options you have, county sheriff departments will always serve papers for you. They often have a separate division or deputy in charge of service. In small towns or rural areas, the sheriff may be the only choice for service. Larger cities usually have commercial process servers as an alternative to the sheriff.

Both types of servers charge fees for service. By law, sheriffs charge a basic service fee of $16 plus mileage (billed at the current state government rate) for travel to and from the defendant. However, a sheriff's service fee can be suspended if you get a fee exemption (see Appendix A for details). Even if you have to pay, sheriffs' service fees are normally cheaper than those of commercial process servers, who often charge upward of $30 for service. On the other hand, commercial process servers may be more persistent in finding and serving defendants.

Whomever you choose, you can often reduce the service fees by having the defendant pick up the service papers at the server's office. This saves the server's mileage fee. It also spares the defendant the possible embarrassment of being served with legal papers at home or work. If the defendant is willing, tell the server that the defendant will pick up the papers, and then have the defendant call the server to arrange for pick-up.

To obtain service by delivery in your area, take the service papers along with your proof of service copy of the Summons and Complaint (MC 01) to the server and ask for service on the defendant. The server will serve the defendant at the address in the captions of your papers. If the defendant can be found at another place, tell the server about the other address.

When the defendant lives in another county or state, you must find a server nearby. After you find one, mail the service papers and your proof of service copy of the Summons and Complaint (MC 01) to the server. Enclose a note asking for service and return of a proof of service (see also "Fees" on page 52 about prepaying an out-of-town server's service fee).

When you're seeking service outside the state of Michigan, you should mention in your note that the server must prove service in the Affidavit of Process server, on the reverse of the proof of service copy of the Summons and Complaint (MC 01). An out-of-state process server must use the affidavit, instead of the Officer Certificate, because only Michigan court officers (such as Michigan sheriffs and their deputies) may use the certificate. In addition, ask the process server to have the notary public affix a seal on the affidavit, since documents with out-of-state notarizations must be sealed.

If all goes as planned, the server will find the defendant and deliver the service papers to him/her. The day of service is the day the server delivers the service papers to the defendant.

More Information

To find sheriffs, look under the county government section for the sheriff department in a telephone directory. For commercial process servers, use a telephone directory for the defendant's area and search under "Process Servers" in the yellow pages.

Or you can find both kinds of process servers through process server trade associations, which provide referrals:

Court Officers, Deputy Sheriffs & Process Servers of Michigan (CODSA) at (989) 831-7644 or www.codsa.com

National Association of Professional Process Servers (NAPPS) at (800) 477-8211 or www.napps.com

United States Process Servers Association (USPSA) at (217) 787-5966 or www.usprocessservers.com

Proving Service by Delivery

After service, the server will prove service on the reverse of the proof of service copy of the Summons and Complaint (MC 01) that you gave the server. For service by Michigan court officers, the proof of service will appear in the Officer Certificate; all other servers must use the Affidavit of Process Server.

After service is proved, the server will return your proof of service copy of the Summons and Complaint (MC 01) to you. Make two copies of this paper and save one for filing later as your proof of service.

Service Problems

In most cases, service by any of the three regular service methods goes smoothly. But certain service methods are best for particular defendants, such as prisoners and military servicemembers. And sometimes you may even have to use alternate service if the defendant is difficult to serve.

Serving Prisoners and Military Servicemembers

Service by mail seems to work best on incarcerated defendants. See "What If My Spouse or I Am Imprisoned?" on page 27 for tips on serving prisoners by mail. Service by mail is also the most effective way to serve military servicemembers, for reasons explained in "What If My Spouse or I Am in the Military?" on page 28.

The regular methods of service work only if the defendant is available for service. But if the defendant is elusive (avoiding service) or has disappeared, you must resort to some form of alternate service. Appendix B has complete instructions and forms for serving elusive or disappeared defendants.

If you're convinced you need alternate service, don't wait too long to seek it. The summons in the Summons and Complaint (MC 01) lasts for 91 days after it's issued (this expiration date should have been inserted by the clerk on the front of the summons). If you fail to complete service within that time, the summons will expire and the clerk will dismiss your case (see below for more about the danger of dismissal).

There is a way to ask the judge for a new summons before the old one expires, but it's a lot of bother. The better way is to use alternate service as soon as it becomes apparent that regular service methods aren't working.

Filing the Proof of Service

Whatever method of service you use, be sure to file the proof of service soon after service is completed. This is important because delay in filing the proof of service can result in dismissal of your divorce.

As mentioned above, a summons expires after 91 days. When there's no proof of service on file after 91 days, the clerk will assume that service has failed and begin dismissal of the case for "no progress." (The clerk should give advance warning of dismissal by sending you a Notice of Intent to Dismiss (MC26).) After dismissal for no progress, you can file a motion asking the judge to reinstate the case. But reinstatement isn't guaranteed, and the judge may deny the motion. In that case, you would have to refile your divorce and start over.

Divorces without minor children are usually finished before the summons expires. But sometimes there can be unexpected delays. To avoid the risk of dismissal, make sure that you file the proof of service quickly, well before the 91-day summons expiration period elapses. Take/send the proof of service, which is on the reverse of your proof of service copy of the Summons and Complaint (MC 01),* plus two copies to the clerk. The clerk will file the original and return two copies to you.

---

*   If alternate service was used, the proof of service is on the reverse of either the MC 304 or MC 307.

1 Filing

Filed with the clerk during filing:

☐ Summons and Complaint   MC 01

☐ Complaint for Divorce   GRP 1

☆ Affidavit and Order, Suspension of Fees/Costs   MC 20

Requested from the clerk during filing (for use later):

☐ Record of Divorce or Annulment   DCH-0838

✦ two strips of caption labels (in Wayne County only)

2 Service

Service papers served on the defendant:

☐ Summons and Complaint   MC 01

☐ Complaint for Divorce   GRP 1

☆ Affidavit and Order, Suspension of Fees/Costs   MC 20

✦ a strip of caption labels (in Wayne County only)

Filed with the clerk soon after service:

☐ proof of service   MC 01

Symbols
▫ regular paper
☆ optional paper
✦ local paper

3 Default

You've filed the divorce and served notice of the case. After several weeks, you're ready for the final part of your divorce, which begins with the default.

A default is important because it means that the defendant isn't contesting the divorce. Until then, you're relying on the defendant's word that the divorce is agreeable. But with the default, your divorce becomes *officially* uncontested, making it impossible for the defendant to re-enter and contest the case without special permission from the court.

Although you may be anxious to get the default, you must wait and see if the defendant responds to your divorce complaint. S/he can respond by filing with the court and sending you either: 1) an Answer to your complaint 2) a motion objecting to the complaint. If the defendant does neither, you can go ahead and apply for a default from the clerk.

To avoid default, the defendant must respond in one of those two ways within the applicable answering period. All answering periods begin the day after the day of service (see "Time" on page 53 for more on computing time periods). The length of answering periods depends on the method of service. The chart on the next page depicts this.

Your copy of the proof of service, which you should have filed earlier, shows the day of service. Use that and the chart to figure the answering period in your case. If the defendant hasn't responded by the end of that answering period, you're ready to get the default.

Answering Periods

Method of service	Day of service	Answering period
Service by acknowledgment	Day defendant takes the service papers from helper	21 days in Michigan or 28 days out of state
Service by mail	Day defendant takes the mailing of the service papers from letter carrier	28 days
Service by delivery	Day server delivers the service papers to defendant	21 days in Michigan or 28 days out of state
Alternate service:		
mailing	Day the service papers are sent	28 days
tacking	Day the service papers are tacked to door	28 days
household delivery	Day the service papers are delivered to person in defendant's household	28 days
publication	Day of final publication of advertisement	Set by judge in MC 307 (a minimum of 28 days after final publication date)
posting	Last day of posting period	Set by judge in MC 307 (a minimum of 28 days after last day of posting period)

Scheduling the Final Hearing

Although your divorce may only be several weeks old when you apply for the default, it's not too early to schedule the final hearing for your case. As required by law, you must appear in court at a final hearing to receive your divorce judgment. Final hearings in divorce cases are usually heard on special days, called motion days, which courts set aside each week or month. During these motion days, judges may hear many final hearings, often at 10- or 15-minute intervals. Nevertheless, judges' motion day schedules fill up quickly, so it's a good idea to schedule your final hearing at the time of the default. If you wait, you risk delaying the conclusion of your divorce.

As previously mentioned, Michigan imposes a 60-day waiting period on divorce cases without minor children (see "How Long Will My Divorce Take?" on page 28 for more on statutory waiting periods). This means that at least 60 days must elapse between the day you filed your divorce (this date is stamped on your Summons and Complaint (MC 01)) and the day of your final hearing.

Although you may want to get your divorce over with sooner, you must observe the waiting period. So when you schedule your final hearing, set it for a day at least 60 days after the day you filed your divorce (see "Time" on page 53 for more about figuring time in days).

Courts use several methods to schedule final hearings in uncontested divorce cases. In many counties, you can schedule a final hearing orally. When you get the default, ask the clerk to schedule a final hearing sometime after the statutory waiting period has expired. The clerk will reserve a time for you on the judge's motion day schedule or calendar (make sure that you make a note of the time and date).

In other counties, you must file a written request for a final hearing. In Wayne County, for example, you must request a final hearing on a special request form known as a praecipe. Wayne County's praecipe is a yellow slip of paper called the At Issue Praecipe for Default Judgment in Domestic Relations Action (#1121), which is available from clerk in room 201 of the Coleman A. Young Municipal Center (CAYMC) (formerly the City-County Bldg.) at 2 Woodward Ave. in Detroit. You file the praecipe with the docket management office in room 770 of the CAYMC. Docket management will have the final hearing scheduled and mail a notice of the time and date to you. Several other counties also use praecipes or similar written forms. If your county is among them, ask the clerk for the particular form and use it as directed.

In some counties, such as Oakland, the clerk will schedule the final hearing for you. These counties typically have computerized case management systems that set final hearings automatically. After the hearing is set, a notice of the time and date will be sent to you.

As you can see, there is a great deal of variation when it comes to scheduling final hearings. In fact, there is probably more variation here than in any other part of divorce procedure. To find out the practice in your county, ask the clerk when you get the default.

Getting the Default

When the defendant has failed to respond to your complaint within the applicable answering period, s/he has defaulted, allowing you to apply to the clerk for a default. The clerk declares or enters the default, but you must prepare the Default (GRP 2) form.

Default and the Military Relief Laws

Glancing at the Default (GRP 2) you'll see some business in the Affidavit section about the defendant's possible service in the military. Why do you have to concern yourself with this issue when you get an uncontested divorce? It's necessary because of a pair of military relief laws (one federal and one state) which protect active-duty servicemembers from hard-to-handle lawsuits, including divorces.

Appendix D has lots more about the military relief laws and their legal impact. In general, the laws provide lawsuit protection to *active-duty* servicemembers, whether as plaintiff or defendant, in the five branches (Army, Navy, Marine Corps, Air Force and Coast Guard) of the U.S. military, and the two branches of the Michigan National Guard (Army National Guard and Air National Guard). See "Military Relief Laws" on page 141 for more about the scope of these laws.

In uncontested divorces, the military relief laws become an issue that must be dealt with in several situations:

Defendant isn't in active-duty military service. By observing the defendant recently, you know that s/he isn't an active-duty servicemember. As a result, you can check the first outdented box in paragraph #4 of the Default (GRP 2), saying that the defendant isn't in active-duty U.S. military service. In addition, check the box that this information is based on your personal knowledge. This will let the court know that the military relief laws don't apply to the defendant.

Defendant is in active-duty military service. You must check the second outdented box in paragraph #4 saying that the defendant is in active-duty military service. See "Divorcing a Defendant-Servicemember" on page 145 for more about dealing with an active-duty defendant-servicemember and the military relief laws protecting them.

One easy way to satisfy these laws is to obtain a waiver of the laws' protections from the defendant. You can get a waiver in the Waiver of Military Relief Rights (GRP 6). Then in paragraph #4 of the Default (GRP 2), check the box indicating that the defendant has waived all lawsuit relief rights, and attach the waiver to the form. See "Waiver of Military Relief Law Rights by the Defendant" on page 146 for more about waiver.

If the defendant-servicemember won't waive, you'll have to deal with the stay remedy of the Soldiers' and Sailors' Civil Relief Act of 1940 (SSCRA). See "Divorcing a Defendant-Servicemember" on page 145 for more about this law. In paragraph #4 of the GRP 2, check the "other" box, and in the space provided say whether or not the defendant has requested a SSCRA stay.

Defendant's (non)military status unknown. The defendant may be elusive or has disappeared, so you don't know personally (hearsay (second-hand information) must be disregarded) whether s/he is in active-duty military service. Or maybe you know that the defendant is in the military, but aren't sure whether s/he is in active or inactive service (reservists frequently change status, especially during a call-up).

Either way, see the sidebox about how to determine the defendant's (non)military status through a military locator service. After you discover

More Information

When you don't know whether or not the defendant is in active-duty military service, you may have to use the military locators to find out. All five service branches have these which provide information about their servicemembers.

Ask for this information in the Request for Certification of Military Status form included in this book. You may have to make requests to all the locators, so fill out the form once and photocopy the form several times. The Request for Certification of Military Status form includes the addresses of the five locator services and the fees they charge for a request.

One problem with any military locator request is that the locators won't give detailed information about troops in deployed units or overseas. But the locators should be able to confirm or deny active-duty status (omitting exact location information), which is all you need for your default application.

the defendant's (non)military status, check the correct boxes in paragraph #4 of the Default (GRP 2) as described above.

Applying for the Default from the Clerk

You can apply to the clerk for the default by mail or personally. Applying in person is best because you can also schedule the final hearing orally or by written request during the visit. Either way, when you apply for the default you should have:

- Default   GRP 2
    - original
    - 2 copies

★ special papers for dealing with a defendant-military ser- vicemember, such as the Waiver of Military Relief Law Rights (GRP 6), (see Appendix D)

✦ praecipe (if needed to schedule the final hearing)

Tell the clerk you want to file a default. The clerk should do the following:

■ Take the Default (GRP 2) and the two copies and complete the Entry section of these papers. File the original Default (GRP 2) and return two copies to you.

★ File any special papers for dealing with a defendant-servicemember and return two copies to you.

✦ After your oral or written request (by praecipe), schedule a final hearing for your case (unless you do it elsewhere or later).

Special Symbols

- ● regular paper
- ■ regular practice
- ★ optional paper or practice
- ✦ local paper or prac- tice

After the Default

Despite the fact that the defendant is removed from the case when you get a default, s/he is due a final notice about the default and upcoming final hearing. By giving this notice, the defendant can't complain later that s/he didn't know about the default and the divorce judgment.

After you get the default, prepare the Notice section of the Notice of Entry of Default and Request for Default Judgment of Divorce (GRP 3). Make a photocopy of the paper and attach a copy of the Default (GRP 2). Send the two papers to the defendant by ordinary first-class mail. If the defendant has disappeared, send the papers to his/her last known address.

If possible, send the Notice of Entry of Default and Request for Default Judgment of Divorce (GRP 3) with attached Default (GRP 2) to the defendant a few days after the default. But if you haven't gotten a final hearing date by then (because in some counties the court will schedule it and mail you a notice), you must wait until the final hearing is scheduled. This might be anytime during the statutory waiting period. But don't wait too long, since the court rules say that the Notice of Entry of Default and Request for Default Judgment of Divorce (GRP 3) must be sent to the defendant *no later than seven days before your final hearing.*

After you send the Notice of Entry of Default and Request for Default Judgment of Divorce (GRP 3) with attached Default (GRP 2) to the defendant, complete the Proof of Mailing section on the original GRP 3 and make a photocopy. Then file/send the Notice of Entry of Default and Request for Default Judgment of Divorce (GRP 3) to the clerk.

STATE OF MICHIGAN Circuit Court - Family Division COUNTY	DEFAULT Application, Affidavit and Entry	CASE NO.

Plaintiff (appearing *in propria persona*):		Defendant:
	v	

APPLICATION

INSERT DAY OF SERVICE

1. As shown by the pro[of of service] file, defendant was served with a summons and complaint on
3-4-89

2. Defendant did not respond to the complaint within 21 days (28 days if served by mail or out of state).

I request the clerk to enter the default of defendant for failure to plead or otherwise defend as provided by law.

Date **4-10-89**   Plaintiff *Darlene A. Lovelace*

AFFIDAVIT

Plaintiff, being sworn, says:

3. Defendant is not a minor or an incompetent person.

☒ is not in active-duty service of the U.S. military. This information is based on
☒ personal knowledge. ☐ attached responses from military locator services

4. Defendant

☐ is in active-duty service of the U.S. military, and ☐ has waived all lawsuit relief rights under the Soldiers' and Sailors' Civil Relief Act of 1940 and/or MCL 32.517 or a similar military relief law from another state in the attached waiver form.
☐ other: _____

CHECK THIS BOX IF THE DEFENDANT IS IN THE MILITARY, AND THEN SEE APPENDIX D ABOUT HOW TO DEAL WITH A DEFENDANT-SERVICE MEMBER

Date **4-10-89**   Plaintiff *Darlene A. Lovelace*

Subscribed and sworn to before me on **4-10-89** , **OJIBWAY** County, Michigan
                                                        Notary public *Loretta Smiley*

My commission expires **1-1-90**

CLERK WILL DATE AND SIGN

ENTRY

The default of defendant is entered for failure to plead or otherwise defend.

Date **4-11-89**   Court clerk *Martha Gee*

GRP 2 (1/04)   DEFAULT, Application, Affidavit and Entry

STATE OF MICHIGAN Circuit Court - Family Division COUNTY	NOTICE OF ENTRY OF DEFAULT AND REQUEST FOR DEFAULT JUDGMENT OF DIVORCE	CASE NO.

Plaintiff (appearing *in propria persona*):

Defendant:

v

NOTICE

> INSERT DATE AND TIME OF HEARING

TO THE DEFENDANT:

1. Your default was entered on ___4-11-89___ , as s[hown on the attached Default.]

2. I will be requesting a default Judgment of Divorce, a[nd] a hearing on this request is scheduled for ___5-7-89___ at ___9:00 A.M.___ in the courtroom of the judge in this case.

3. At the hearing, the judge may enter a Judgment of Divorce granting the relief I requested in my Complaint for Divorce and/or grant other relief.

Date __4-12-89__

Plaintiff _Darlene A. Lovelace_

PROOF OF MAILING

On the date below, I sent copies of this notice and the Default entered in this case to defendant at his/her address in the caption above by ordinary first-class mail.

I declare that the statement above is true to the best of my information, knowledge and belief.

Date __4-12-89__

Plaintiff _Darlene A. Lovelace_

GRP 3   (1/04)   NOTICE OF/ DEFAULT/ REQUEST FOR DEFAULT JUDGMENT OF DIVORCE

Request for Certification of Military Status

TO:

Army Worldwide Locator
U.S. Army Enlisted Records and Evaluation Center
8899 E. 56th St.
Indianapolis, IN 46249-5301
Fee: $3.50 payable by check or money to "Finance Officer"

World Wide Locator
Bureau of Naval Personnel
Pers-324D
2 Navy Annex
Washington, DC 20370-3240
Fee: $3.50 payable by check or money to "U.S. Treasurer"

Headquarters U.S. Marine Corps
Personnel Management Support Branch (MMSB-17)
2008 Elliot Rd.
Quantico, VA 22134-5030
Fee: $3.50 payable by check or money to "U.S. Treasurer"

HQ AFPC/MSIMD
550 C St. West, Suite 50
Randolph AFB, TX 78150-4752
Fee: $3.50 payable by check or money order to "DAO-DE RAFB"

Coast Guard Locator Service
Commanding Officer (RAS)
444 SE Quincy St.
Topeka, KS 66683-3591
Fee: $3.50 payable by check or money order to "U.S. Treasurer"

RE:

Case name ___LOVELACE v. LOVELACE___

Case number ___89-00501-DO___

Full name of defendant ___DUDLEY ERNEST LOVELACE___

Defendant's date of birth___6-15-64___

Defendant's social security number ___379-10-5567___

Defendant's rank and service number (if known)___

Defendant's last duty assignment (if known) ___

Defendant's last military address (if known) ___

 I am the plaintiff in the above divorce case seeking a default judgment of divorce against the defendant. I must know whether or not the defendant is currently in the active duty of your branch of the U.S. military service, to comply with the Soldiers' and Sailors' Civil Relief Act of 1940 and/or Michigan Compiled Law 32.517 or a similar military relief law from another state.

 Please respond with a certificate of the defendant's (non)military status, unit of assignment and military address, if any, as soon as possible. If the defendant is overseas or in a deployed unit, please certify whether the defendant is or is not in active-duty service and omit the other requested information from your response.

 A self-addressed stamped envelope is enclosed for your response. A certification fee is also enclosed, but if I qualify for a fee waiver (as spouse), please refund my payment.

Date _3-15-89_

Signature _Darlene A. Lovelace_

Name _DARLENE A. LOVELACE_

Address _121. S. MAIN_

LAKE CITY, MI 48800

Telephone: _(517)772-0000_

4 Final Hearing

The final hearing comes at the end of your divorce. This hearing is held in court before the judge assigned to your case. You must attend the hearing and give some brief testimony to get a Judgment of Divorce (GRP 4), which decides all the divorce issues. Your divorce becomes final immediately after the hearing, when the judgment is filed.

Final Divorce Papers

The final hearing requires some preparation. A few days before the hearing, you should prepare the Judgment of Divorce (GRP 4) and any other final divorce papers you need. The Judgment of Divorce (GRP 4) is by far the most important divorce paper. The judgment ends the marriage, divides property, deals with alimony and may change a wife's name.

Although the Judgment of Divorce (GRP 4) is the court's order, you must prepare it for the court. For guidance, see the sample judgment at the end of this section and the additional judgment provisions in Appendix F.

Besides the Judgment of Divorce (GRP 4), your final divorce papers include the Record of Divorce or Annulment (DCH-0838). You probably got this form from the clerk when you filed the divorce. If not, you can obtain it from the clerk anytime. To prepare the Record of Divorce or Annulment (DCH-0838) for filing, answer questions #1-16 and #19-20. In Wayne County only, you must prepare an extra paper: the Certificate of Conformity for Domestic Relations Order or Judgment (1225). This paper tells the judge that your divorce judgment satisfies all legal requirements.

Preparing for the Final Hearing

Before you appear in court for your final hearing, you may want to prepare the testimony for the hearing. Since you don't have a lawyer to question you during the hearing, you must give the testimony in a monologue. This is a little more difficult than testifying by answering questions. Therefore, you might find it helpful to plan your testimony beforehand.

One way you can do that is by using a script to organize your testimony. By preparing a testimony script, you should be able to memorize the bulk of your testimony. You can also take your testimony script with you to the final hearing and rely on it a bit if your memory fails while you're on the witness stand (using written materials to jog a witness' memory is called "refreshing the recollection," and is permitted by the rules of evidence).

Luckily, the testimony you give during a final hearing is usually quite brief; in most cases it's simply a repetition of the information contained in the divorce complaint. Some courts even skip the testimony entirely, and merely have you swear that the contents of the complaint are true.

You give all the testimony for your hearing; you don't need any testimony from the defendant or other witnesses. In fact, the defendant will probably be absent. Defendants have the right to attend final hearings, but cannot directly participate because of their default. Thus, defendants seldom attend final hearings in uncontested divorce cases.

On the other hand, having the defendant at the final hearing can be helpful to the judge. With the defendant present, the judge can ask him/her about such things as complicated property divisions. Defendant-wives who want their names changed must also attend their final hearings to receive name changes.

Special Symbols

● regular paper

■ regular practice

★ optional paper or practice

✦ local paper or practice

Before the Final Hearing

When you attend the final hearing, it's a good idea to bring your file with all your divorce papers to the final hearing. If you haven't kept a file, at least bring the following items:

● Judgment of Divorce   GRP 4
  ● original
  ● 2 copies

● Record of Divorce or Annulment   DCH-0838

● testimony script

✦ Certificate of Conformity for Domestic Relations   1225
  Order or Judgment (in Wayne County only)
  ● original
  ● 2 copies

Attending the Final Hearing

When you go to the courthouse for the final hearing, arrive early so you can take care of any final details. Clerks often want you to check in with them to let them know that you are present and ready for the final hearing. In some counties, the clerk will give your case file to you to take to the courtroom. But in most counties the clerk will send the file to the courtroom ahead of time.

You should go to your judge's courtroom before the final hearing is scheduled to begin and wait in the visitor's section in back (see "Court Appearances" on page 54 for more about how courts conduct hearings, and how you should conduct yourself during a hearing in court). As your case is called, identify yourself, step forward and take a place at one of the tables. When the judge tells you to proceed, offer your Judgment of Divorce (GRP 4) and say you're ready to give the testimony.

After you take the witness stand and are sworn in, give the testimony as you have planned it. If you omit something important, the judge may question you briefly to complete the testimony. When your testimony is finished, ask the judge to enter your Judgment of Divorce (GRP 4). If the judgment is satisfactory, the judge will sign the original Judgment of Divorce (GRP 4) and maybe some copies.

If the judge objects to your judgment, s/he should tell you what the problem is. It may be something you can fix on the spot. If not, ask the judge for an opportunity to correct the judgment later. The court rules permit you to submit a corrected judgment to the judge within 14 days after the final hearing. If you get that chance, make any necessary modifications of your Judgment of Divorce (GRP 4) and take it to the judge's office. S/he should sign it there and you won't need another final hearing.

But if something really goes wrong at your final hearing, ask the judge for an adjournment of the hearing. Find out what the problem is and, after you fix it, reschedule another final hearing. If you reschedule the final hearing, you must also give the defendant notice of the new final hearing in the Notice of Entry of Default and Request for Default Judgment of Divorce (GRP 3). This notice must be given at least seven days before the new final hearing takes place (see "After the Default" on page 81 for more about giving this notice).

Filing the Final Divorce Papers

After the final hearing, file your final divorce papers with the clerk. Filing the papers quickly is important because, according to paragraph #12 of the Judgment of Divorce (GRP 4a), your divorce only becomes final when you file the judgment. At that time, your marriage is ended and all the other provisions of the judgment take effect.

In a few counties, you can file your final divorce papers (and pay the judgment fee) with the courtroom clerk during the final hearing. But in most counties, you must return to the clerk's office, where the clerk will:

■ File the Judgment of Divorce (GRP 4) and return two copies to you.

■ Take the Record of Divorce or Annulment (DCH-0838).

✦ In Wayne County only, file the Certificate of Conformity for Domestic Relations Order or Judgment (1225) and return two copies to you.

Before you leave the clerk's office you may want to obtain several *certified* copies of the Judgment of Divorce (GRP 4). These copies can be helpful in carrying out the judgment's property division or verifying a name change. See "After Your Divorce" on page 97 for more about these issues. Bring extra money for certified copies because the clerk charges $10 for issuing a certified copy plus $1 for each page of the document.

After the Final Hearing

Naturally, the defendant must know what the Judgment of Divorce (GRP 4) says because its provisions affect him/her. After the final hearing, the clerk should send the defendant a brief notice that a judgment was issued. However, the clerk doesn't send a copy of the Judgment of Divorce (GRP 4) itself to the defendant along with this notice. That's your responsibility.

You must send the judgment to the defendant within seven days of the final hearing. To do that, send a copy of the Judgment of Divorce (GRP 4) to the defendant by ordinary first-class mail. If the defendant has disappeared, send it to his/her last known address. After the mailing, prepare the Proof of Mailing (MC 302) and make two copies. Then file/send the original to the clerk.

STATE OF MICHIGAN Circuit Court - Family Division COUNTY	JUDGMENT OF DIVORCE Page 1 of **2** pages	CASE NO.

Plaintiff (appearing *in propria persona*):

v

Defendant:

Date of hearing **5-7-89**   Judge **LESTER TUBBS**

After the defendant's default, **IT IS ORDERED:**

1. **DIVORCE:** The parties are divorced.

2. **CHILDREN:** There ☐ are ☒ are not   children of the parties or born during the
   are under 18 or adult and entitled to support.

☒ 3. **NAME CHANGE:** Wife's last name is changed to _**ALBRIGHT**_

> USE FOR WIFE'S NAME CHANGE

4. **SPOUSAL SUPPORT:** Spousal support is
   ☒ not granted for   ☒ wife. ☒ husband.
   ☐ reserved for   ☐ wife. ☐ husband.
   ☐ granted later in the judgment for ☐ wife. ☐ husband.

> SEE "ALIMONY PROVISIONS" IN APPENDIX F FOR MORE ON SPOUSAL SUPPORT (ALIMONY)

5. **PROPERTY DIVISION:**

A. **Real property:**   ☐ The parties do not own any real property.
   (Land and buildings)   ☒ Real property is divided elsewhere in this judgment.

All real property owned by the parties in joint tenancy or tenancy by the entirety is converted to te
cy in common, unless this judgment provides otherwise.

B. **Personal property:**   ☒ Each party is awarded the personal property in his or her posses
   (All other property)   ☒ Personal property is divided elsewhere in this judgment.

6. **STATUTORY RIGHTS:** All interests of the parties in the property of the other, now owned or later
   acquired, under MCL 700.2201-700.2405, are extinguished, including those known as dower
   under MCL 558.1-558.29.

7. **BENEFICIARY RIGHTS:** The rights each party has to the pro
   insurance, endowments or annuities upon the life of the other as a
   ment during or in anticipation of marriage, are ☒ extinguished. ☐

> SEE "PROPERTY DIVISION PROVISIONS" IN APPENDIX F FOR MORE ON PROPERTY DIVISIONS
> CHECK BOXES AS THEY APPLY

8. **RETIREMENT BENEFITS:** Any rights of either party in any pens
   benefit of the other, whether these rights are vested or unvested, a
   ☒ extinguished. ☐ awarded later in the judgment.

> SEE "PROPERTY DIVISION PROVISIONS" IN APPENDIX F FOR MORE ON DIVIDING RETIREMENT BENEFITS

9. **DOCUMENTATION:** Each party shall promptly and properly execute and de
   documents to carry out the terms of this judgment. A certified copy of this jud
   recorded with the register of deeds in any county of this state where property

10. **PRIOR ORDERS:** Except as otherwise provided in this judgment, any nonfinal orders or injunc-
    tions entered in this action are terminated.

☐ 11. **SUSPENDED FEES AND COSTS:** The previously suspended fees and costs in this case of
    _____ shall be ☐ paid by ☐ plaintiff ☐ defendant   to the clerk. ☐ waived finally.

12. **EFFECTIVE DATE OF JUDGMENT:** This judgment shall become effective immediately after it is
    signed by the judge and filed with the clerk.

GRP 4a (1/04)   JUDGMENT OF DIVORCE, page 1

Bombardier 4x4
4wheeler

STATE OF MICHIGAN Circuit Court - Family Division COUNTY	JUDGMENT OF DIVORCE Final of 2 pages	CASE NO.

Plaintiff: v   **Defendant:**

IT IS ALSO ORDERED:

13.

14.

ETC.

INCLUDE ADDITIONAL JUDGMENT PROVISIONS HERE AS NEEDED

CHECK THESE BOXES TO CLOSE THE CASE

JUDGE WILL DATE AND SIGN AT FINAL HEARING

... judgment ☒ resolves ☐ does not resolve the
...pending claim in this case, and ☒ closes ☐ does
...close the case, except to the extent jurisdiction is
...tained by law.

Reviewed by FO?

Date   5-7-89   Judge *Lester Jubbs*

GRP 4e (1/04)   JUDGMENT OF DIVORCE, final page

Testimony

1) My name is [full name] , my address is [address], and I am the plaintiff in this case.

2) I was married to the defendant on **SEPT 1, 1985** at **LAKE CITY, MICHIGAN** by a person authorized to
   Date and place of marriage
   perform marriages.

3) Before the marriage, my/[my wife's] name was **DARLENE ANN ALBRIGHT** .
   Wife's former name

4) I filed my complaint for divorce on **MARCH 1, 1989** . Before I filed the complaint, I had resided in Michigan since
   Filing date
   1970 and in this county since **1970** .
   State residency   County residency

5) As I said in my complaint, there has been a breakdown in our marriage relationship to the extent the objects of matrimony
   have been destroyed because **WE COULD NEVER GET ALONG TOGETHER** and there remains no
   Brief facts to support grounds
   reasonable likelihood that our marriage can be preserved because **WE ARE TOTALLY INCOMPATIBLE** .
   Brief facts to support grounds

6) The defendant and I have no minor children, and I/[my wife] am not now pregnant.

7) I am working at **A RESTAURANT AS A WAITRESS** and am able to support myself.
   Source of support

8) We own some **CLOTHING AND HOUSEHOLD GOODS** that we have split between us. We have also agreed that
   General description of personal property
   the defendant is to give me **A 1984 DODGE ARIES** and I will pay off the debt on it.
   Specific items of personal property transferred in judgment

9) We also own **A HOUSE IN LAKE CITY** worth around **$35,000**
   Description of any real property   Value
   We have agreed to **SELL IT, PAY OFF THE MORTGAGE AND SPLIT THE REST**
   Manner of division

   USE WHEN APPLICABLE

10) I would like my former name of **ALBRIGHT** back.
    Wife's name change

11) My court fees were suspended when I filed this divorce. Since then, **I AM STILL GETTING AFDC AND MY HUSBAND IS UNEMPLOYED**
    Current financial condition

12) Does the court have any questions?

3-8-00 Property
12-14-00 Home Purchased
1-29-03 Refinaced

STATE OF MICHIGAN
THIRD JUDICIAL CIRCUIT
WAYNE COUNTY
Penobscot Bldg. 645 Griswold Ave. Detroit, MI 48226

CERTIFICATE OF CONFORMITY
FOR DOMESTIC RELATIONS
ORDER OR JUDGMENT

CASE NO.

313-224-5372

PLAINTIFF'S NAME

v.

DEFENDANT'S NAME

I certify the attached Order or Judgment as presented for entry to be in full conformity with the requirements set forth by statute, INCLUDING A PROVISION FOR IMMEDIATE INCOME WITHHOLDING (WHICH SHALL BE IMPLEMENTED BY THE FRIEND OF THE COURT), THE PAYER'S SOCIAL SECURITY NUMBER AND THE NAME AND ADDRESS OF HIS/HER SOURCE OF INCOME IF KNOWN , UNLESS OTHERWISE ORDERED BY THE COURT, and with Michigan Court Rules 3.201 and following, and if applicable, includes all provisions of the Friend of the Court recommendation or is in conformity with the decision of

_____ rendered on the _____ day of

_____ , 19 _____ .

5-5-89
Date

Darlene A. Lovelace
Attorney / Bar No.
PLAINTIFF

Instructions :   Please sign and present this Certificate to the Court Clerk when the Order or Judgment is presented for entry. If an ex parte interim order is being presented to the Judge, please complete the "Certificate on Behalf of Plaintiff regarding Ex Parte Interim Support Order" and follow Local Court Rule 3.206.

USE THIS FORM
IN WAYNE
COUNTY ONLY.

#1225 (7/95) CERTIFICATE OF CONFORMITY FOR DOMESTIC RELATIONS ORDER OR JUDGMENT

Approved, SCAO		CASE NO.
STATE OF MICHIGAN **JUDICIAL DISTRICT** **JUDICIAL CIRCUIT**	**PROOF OF MAILING**	Court telephone no.

Court address

Plaintiff(s)	v	Defendant(s)

On the date below I sent by first class mail a copy of ———— JUDGMENT OF DIVORCE ————

to: Names and addresses

DUDLEY LOVELACE
900 S. MAPLE
LAKE CITY, MI 48800

I declare that the statements above are true to the best of my information, knowledge and belief.

DARLENE A. LOVELACE
Name (typed)

5-8-89
Date

Darlene A. Lovelace
Signature

MC 302 (5/88) PROOF OF MAILING

3 Default

Filed with the clerk when the default is received:

GRP 2

☐ Default

☆ Waiver of Military Relief Law Rights, if defendant is in active-duty military service and is willing to waive military
relief law rights

GRP 6

✧ praecipe or other written request for a final hearing

Filed with the clerk after the default:

☐ Notice of Entry of Default and Request for Default Judgment of Divorce

GRP 3

4 Final Hearing

Filed with the clerk after the final hearing:

GRP 4

☐ Judgment of Divorce

DCH-0838

☐ Record of Divorce or Annulment

✧ Certificate of Conformity for Domestic Relations Order
or Judgment (in Wayne County only)

1225

Filed with the clerk after service of the final papers on the defendant:

MC 302

☐ Proof of Mailing

Symbols

▫ regular paper
☆ optional paper
✧ local paper

After Your Divorce

Although your divorce is over, there's still some work to do. The Judgment of Divorce (GRP 4) takes legal effect at filing, but you must carry out several judgment provisions. What's more, the end of your marriage may require changes in your will, powers of attorney, insurance, retirement benefits, etc.

Transferring Property

The Judgment of Divorce (GRP 4) divided your property, but it's your responsibility to transfer ownership of the property.

Ownership of real property must be transferred by deed. For transfers between ex-spouses, a simple form of deed called a quit claim deed is customarily used. Lawyers or real estate brokers can prepare these for a small fee.

If your ex-spouse is uncooperative or unavailable for transfer, you can sometimes use the divorce judgment to transfer ownership of real property yourself. To use the judgment this way, it must describe the property in detail (see "Property Division Provisions" in Appendix F for more about describing property using legal descriptions or identification numbers). You must also have an official certified copy of the judgment for the transfer. These are available from the clerk for a small fee.

You can transfer Michigan real property by recording a certified copy of the divorce judgment with the register of deeds for the county where the property is located. This transfer method isn't available for out-of-state real property.

To Obtain

A certified copy of your divorce judgment, go to the clerk of the court that granted your divorce.

There is a $10 fee for issuing a certified copy, plus $1 for each page of the document.

Personal property without titles (clothing, household goods, etc.) can be transferred by simply changing possession of the items. But both possession and title must be transferred for personal property with titles (stocks, bonds, motor vehicles, etc.). Stocks and bonds can be transferred through the designated transfer agent (usually a bank but sometimes the issuing company itself).

Transfer titles to motor vehicles through a secretary of state office by applying for a new title after the current owner has signed off on the back of the old certificate of title.

If the owner refuses to cooperate, you can use a certified copy of the divorce judgment for transfer of title. When you apply for a new title, submit a certified copy of the judgment, and you won't need your ex's signature on the old certificate of title.

Debts

You may have already closed or frozen joint accounts (see "Does My Property Need Protection?" on page 36 for more about handling joint accounts during divorce). If you haven't, do this at once. Otherwise, your ex can add new joint debt after the divorce for which you may be liable.

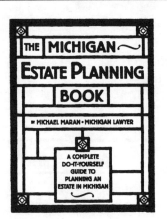
Estate Planning

Paragraphs #7 and #8 of the Judgment of Divorce (GRP 4a) end all claims you and your ex-spouse have against each other's life insurance and retirement benefits (unless you preserved these rights in the judgment).

Despite these provisions, you should contact your insurance agent and/or retirement plan administrator and revoke any designations of your spouse as beneficiary. Because of a legal peculiarity, a divorce judgment's revocations aren't always effective, making individual revocation necessary. As you make the revocation, it's a good time to designate new beneficiaries.

Paragraph #6 of the Judgment of Divorce (GRP 4a) cuts off all rights that spouses have in their partners' estates (see "Do I Really Want to End My Marriage?" on page 19 for a description of these rights). And although the judgment doesn't mention it, Michigan law says that divorce automatically revokes: 1) all rights that spouses have been given in each other's will 2) appointment of a spouse as personal representative.

But besides those selected will provisions, divorce doesn't touch any other parts of a will. The will, minus the provisions benefiting an ex-spouse, remains in force. All the same, you should carefully review your will after divorce. The removal of your ex-spouse from the will may have upset your scheme of property distribution and appointments. After review, you may decide that your will needs revision or even replacement.

These days, some people have living (*inter vivos*) trusts instead of wills. If you have one, with your ex as trustee and/or beneficiary, you'll probably want to amend the trust and remove your ex.

You might have already revoked a durable power of attorney for financial affairs naming your ex-spouse as agent. If not, you may want to revoke it now. Simply give or send a written notice telling your ex that you are revoking the power of attorney and his/her powers under it. Make sure you keep a copy of the revocation.

In 1990, Michigan created a special health care power of attorney allowing you to designate an agent, called a patient advocate, to make health care decisions, including the termination of life-sustaining treatment, on your behalf. Like durable powers of attorney, spouses who make these arrangements often name each other as patient advocates.

The health care power of attorney law helpfully provides that a designation of a spouse as patient advocate is suspended while a divorce is pending. Then, when the divorce judgment is filed, the health care power of attorney is automatically revoked, unless you named a successor patient advocate. In that case, the power of attorney remains in effect with the successor as patient advocate.

More Information

If they don't have good coverage of their own, ex-spouses should look into these coverage options:

COBRA-coverage. A 1985 law, the Consolidated Omnibus Budget Reconciliation Act, or COBRA for short, can provide health care coverage. Immediately after divorce, COBRA allows you to obtain health care coverage for you and/or dependent children from your ex's employer-provided group plan (if the employer has 20 or more employees), which can last for a maximum of three years. What's more, you don't have to show medical insurability to get COBRA-coverage, so for example, you can get coverage immediately when you have high medical risks or pre-existing conditions.

One drawback to COBRA: You may have to pay the plan premiums (both the employer and employee shares) yourself. But fortunately, the premiums must be charged at group rates, which are usually lower than individual rates.

County health plans. Ingham County has devised a health plan for those without health care coverage. It provides coverage for doctor's visits and prescription drugs, but not hospitalization. Other counties have signed on to Ingham's plan extending it all over the state.

Hill-Burton program. Years ago, the federal government provided loans and grants to many hospitals for construction and modernization under the Hill-Burton Act. In return, these Hill-Burton hospitals promised to provide a certain amount of reduced-cost or free care to low-income patients. Many hospitals have fulfilled their Hill-Burton obligations, and don't have to provide this care any more; others still must (as of 2001, there were still around 50 Hill-Burton health care facilities in Michigan). If you are hospitalized at a Hill-Burton hospital you may qualify for uncompensated care.

Individual policy. You can go into the open market and obtain an individual health plan. This type of care can be expensive, but you can limit the cost by choosing higher deductibles and co-payments.

Health Care Coverage

With the high cost of health care these days, health care coverage is vital. The sidebox above describes some coverage options if you lack employer-provided or your own coverage.

If you decide to obtain COBRA-coverage through your ex-spouse's employer, contact his/her employee benefits office within 60 days after your divorce judgment is granted. Wait longer and you can lose the right to obtain health plan coverage this way.

Name Change

If you changed your name during the divorce, you must report the name change to the following agencies and offices, so documents issued by them can be revised:

- Michigan Secretary of State (driver's license and voter registration)
- Social Security Administration (social security card)
- passport acceptance agency (U.S. Post Office, county clerk, etc.) (passport)
- financial institutions (bank accounts, credit cards, etc.)
- insurance companies (life, disability and health insurance policies and documents)
- heath care providers (health care files and documents at doctor, dentist, etc.)
- utilities (accounts with utilities, telephone companies, cable television, etc.)
- employer (employee benefits documents)
- schools and alumni associations (school records, alumni directories, etc.)
- airlines (frequent flier programs)

More Information

About enforcement of the property division, or enforcement or modification of the alimony provision, in a divorce judgment, plus information about post-divorce name change, tax problems, debt and credit issues, order *After the Divorce: A Do-It-Yourself Guide to Enforcing or Modifying a Divorce Judgment in Michigan*, using the order form at the front of this book.

Typically, you must visit many of these offices and agencies in person to change your name; it's difficult to make the change over the telephone or Internet. Many of these agencies and offices also require evidence of your name change. For proof, bring certified copies of the Judgment of Divorce (GRP 4).

Credit Problems

Today, in our consumer economy credit is more important than ever. As always, lenders look at credit reports (tracking a person's borrowing and payment habits) when making lending decisions. But more and more, auto and homeowner insurance companies are using credit histories to determine insurability and premiums, and mortgage companies base interest rates on creditworthiness.

After divorce, many women suddenly discover that they can't get credit because they have no credit history. A woman may lose credit if her credit was reported in her previous married name. Even women who don't change their names may suffer a loss of credit it they got credit through their husbands' credit reports.

The solution to these credit woes is building a credit history in your own name. If you had credit under your former married name, you can add this information to your credit file. Joint accounts with your husband may have been reported in your husband's name only (all joint accounts opened after June 1, 1977, are supposed to reported in both spouses' names). If so, you can sometimes persuade credit reporting agencies to add these credit references to your file.

In addition, you can apply for new credit from banks, retailers and other creditors to build a credit history. A federal law, the Equal Credit Opportunity Act (ECOA), bars creditors from canceling old credit accounts you had during marriage if you still meet their lending standards (you may have to submit new information to prove your creditworthiness). The ECOA also guarantees creditworthy persons access to credit regardless of sex or marital status, and outlaws various discriminatory credit practices.

As you build a credit history, make sure you pay your bills on time, because this factor has the biggest impact on credit. It's also smart to have a good mix of credit, with both revolving (credit cards, charge accounts) and installment (mortgages, loans) debt.

One thing to avoid are credit repair services. These firms often charge a lot for meager results. Even worse, they can sometimes commit illegal practices for which you can be liable.

More Information

Credit agencies receive credit information from lenders and merchants, compile this information into credit reports and sell these to lenders and others. To check on your credit status, get copies of your credit reports from the three main credit reporting agencies:

Equifax: P.O. Box 105873, Atlanta, GA 30348, (800) 685-1111 or www.equifax.com

Experian: P.O. Box 2104, Allen, TX 75013, (888) 397-3742 or www.experian.com

TransUnion: TransUnion LLC, Consumer Disclosure Center, P.O. Box 1000, Chester, PA 19022, (800) 888-4213 or www.transunion.com

Each report is around $10, but consumers are entitled to one free report per year from each company.

Each agency's report has different credit information. To compare them all, you can get a combined three-in-one report. TrueCredit.com offers a combined report for around $35. TransUnion also provides referrals to TrueCredit.

Be careful about ordering seemingly free credit reports on the Internet. Many of these offers appear to be free, but have hidden fees and costs.

Ask for the brochures "Women and Credit Histories" and "Equal Credit Opportunity" from:

Federal Trade Commission
Attn: Ed Bush
6th & Pennsylvania Ave. N.W.
Washington, D.C. 20580

Appendices

Appendix A: Fee Exemption

Michigan law exempts some poor people from payment of the court fees of their divorces (see "How Much Will My Divorce Cost?" on page 29 for a description of these fees). If you qualify, you can get an exemption from payment of the filing fee and any motion fees. You can also get an exemption from the service fee when you must use: 1) an official server (such as a sheriff for service by delivery; or a sheriff, policeman, or court officer for alternate service by posting) 2) publication for alternate service. Otherwise, you must pay the service fee yourself for service by mail or service by delivery using a commercial process server.

Who can qualify for a fee exemption? The court rules say that persons receiving "any form of public assistance" are automatically entitled to a fee exemption. The rules don't define public assistance, but presumably it includes the main public welfare programs: 1) Family Independence Program (FIP) payments (formerly AFDC) 2) Temporary Assistance to Needy Families (TANF) 3) Supplemental Security Income (SSI) 4) food stamps 5) Medicaid.

In addition, the court rules say that indigent persons may qualify for fee exemptions. Indigent is just another word for poor. In Michigan, judges determine indigency on a case-by-case basis after they have reviewed applicants' financial information(income and assets versus obligations).

The fee exemption rules apply to all types of lawsuits, but there is a special rule for divorce cases. Although you and your spouse may be separated and financially independent, you're still treated as a family unit for fee exemption purposes. If you cannot pay the fees, but your spouse can, s/he may be ordered to pay them for you. If neither of you can pay the fees, because of: 1) receipt of public assistance 2) indigency, both of you are exempt from payment.

Obtaining a Fee Exemption

Obtaining a fee exemption is a two-step procedure: 1) initial suspension of fees when a divorce is filed 2) final exemption (or payment) of the fees at the end of the divorce. To get fees suspended initially, prepare the Affidavit section of the Affidavit and Order, Suspension of Fees/Costs (MC 20), and submit it to the clerk when you file your initial divorce papers.

A fee exemption request itself is a kind of motion for which a motion fee would normally be paid. However, the court rules say that no motion fee is due for fee exemption requests.

The clerk gives automatic fee exemptions to plaintiffs receiving public assistance. If you claim indigency, the clerk will pass the Affidavit and Order, Suspension of Fees/Costs (MC 20) onto the judge for review. If the judge agrees that you're indigent, s/he will order a fee suspension on the reverse of the Affidavit and Order, Suspension of Fees/Costs (MC 20). A denial of your application would be indicated in the same place.

If your application is successful, you won't have to pay any fees during your divorce. However, the court will review your fee exemption at the end of the divorce. At that time, it will take another look at your financial condition and make a final decision about the fees.

During your testimony at the final hearing, you must mention that your fees were suspended at the beginning of the divorce. The judge will then re-examine your financial condition and either: 1) order you or your spouse to pay the fees 2) give you and your spouse a final waiver from payment of the fees. The same standards apply then as before; those on public assistance get an automatic exemption, while those claiming indigency must cite facts to prove it. To prove indigency, you should give extra testimony about your present financial condition.

Whatever the judge decides, you can provide for payment of the suspended fees (by you or the defendant) or a final fee waiver in paragraph #11 of the Judgment of Divorce (GRP 4a). Insert the amount of the suspended fees and check the correct box.

The form:

Original - Court
1st copy - Applicant

2nd copy - Opposing party
PROBATE OSM CODE: OSF

CASE NO.

Approved, SCAO

STATE OF MICHIGAN
JUDICIAL DISTRICT
JUDICIAL CIRCUIT
COUNTY PROBATE

**AFFIDAVIT AND ORDER
SUSPENSION OF FEES/COSTS**

Court telephone no.

Court address

Plaintiff/Petitioner name, address, and telephone no.

v

Defendant/Respondent name, address, and telephone no.

Plaintiff's/Petitioner's attorney, bar no., address, and telephone no.

Defendant's/Respondent's attorney, bar no., address, and telephone no.

☐ Probate   In the matter of _____

NOTE: Requests for waiver/suspension of transcript costs must be made separately by motion.

AFFIDAVIT   DARLENE A. LOVELACE
Name

1. The attached pleading is to be filed with the court by or on behalf of applicant, who is ☒ plaintiff/petitioner. ☐ defendant/respondent.

2. The applicant is entitled to and asks the court for suspension of fees and costs in the action for the following reason:

$ 400 per MONTH Case No.: V1336092B

☒ a. S/he is currently receiving public assistance:

☒ b. S/he is unable to pay those fees and costs because of indigency, based on the following facts:

INCOME: 10,000 PANCAKES, 111 M-78, LAKE CITY, MI 48800
Employer name and address
1 YR. $250 $225 per ☒ week. ☐ month. ☐ two we
Length of employment Average gross pay Average net pay

ASSETS: State value of car, home, bank deposits, bonds, stocks, etc.
HOUSEHOLD GOODS $1,000
CAR $1,000

OBLIGATIONS: Itemize monthly rent, installment payments, mortgage payments, child support, etc.
CAR PAYMENT $75 FOOD $200
RENT $250

☐ 3. (in domestic relations cases only) The applicant is entitled to an order requiring his/her spouse to pay attorney re

REIMBURSEMENT: It is understood that the court may order the applicant to pay the fees and costs when the reason f waiver or suspension no longer exists.

Darlene A. Lovelace
Affiant signature

Subscribed and sworn to before me on 2-28-89 Date OJIBWAY County, Michigan.

My commission expires: 1-1-90 Date Signature: Loretta Smiley Deputy clerk/Register/Notary public

(SEE REVERSE SIDE FOR ORDER)

MC 20 (6/03) **AFFIDAVIT AND ORDER, SUSPENSION OF FEES/COSTS**

Margin notes:
- COMPLETE 2a. IF YOU ARE RECEIVING PUBLIC ASSISTANCE
- COMPLETE 2b. INSTEAD IF YOU ARE CLAIMING INDIGENCY. PRISONERS CLAIMING INDIGENCY SHOULD CHECK BOX 2b., SKIP REST OF THE SECTION, AND ATTACH CERTIFIED COPY OF THEIR INSTITUTIONAL ACCOUNT FOR PRIOR YEAR
- IF YOU MUST USE AN OFFICIAL SERVER, OR MUST GET ALTERNATE SERVICE BY PUBLICATION, EXPLAIN THAT ON A SHEET ATTACHED TO THIS FORM

CERTIFICATION OF ATTORNEY

1. I have reviewed the affidavit of indigency, and I certify that its contents are true to the best of my information, knowledge, and belief.

2. I will bring to the court's attention the matter of suspended costs and fees and the availability of funds to pay them before any disposition is entered. I will report at that time any changes in the information contained in the affidavit of indigency or any other information regarding the affiant's financial status or alterations of the fee arrangement.

Date _____

Attorney signature _____

Attorney name (type or print) _____

Bar no. _____

CERTIFICATION BY PERSON OTHER THAN PARTY

1. I have personal knowledge of the facts appearing in the affidavit.

2. The person in whose behalf the petition is filed is unable to sign it because of

☐ minority: _____
        Date of birth

Relationship: _____   ☐ other disability: _____
                                                                    Nature of disability

_____

Date _____

(speech bubble: LEAVE CERTIFICATIONS BLANK)

(speech bubble: JUDGE WILL SUSPEND FEES OR DENY FEE SUSPENSION BELOW)

Affiant signature _____

Affiant name (type or print) _____

Address _____

City, state, zip _____

Telephone no. _____

IT IS ORDERED: **ORDER**

☒ 1. Fees and costs in this action required by law or court rule are waived/suspended until further order of the court. Before any final disposition or discontinuance is entered, the moving party shall bring the fee and costs suspension to the attention of the judge for final disposition.

☐ 2. The applicant's spouse shall pay the fees and costs required by law or court rule.

☐ 3. This application is denied.

3-1-89
Date _____

Lester Tubbs
Judge _____

Bar no. _____

(speech bubble: JUDGE WILL DATE AND SIGN)

Appendix B:
Alternate Service

The regular service methods of service by acknowledgment, mail and delivery are very effective when defendants are available for service. But if the defendant is hiding from service (an elusive defendant), or has disappeared entirely (a disappeared defendant), you must use another method of service.

Luckily, the court rules authorize alternate service on elusive and disappeared defendants. By using alternate service, your divorce can go ahead normally, just as if you had served the defendant by one of the regular service methods.

Forms of Alternate Service

Alternate service can take several forms including: 1) mailing 2) tacking (attaching papers to a door) 3) household delivery (delivering papers to an adult in the defendant's household) 4) publication (with or without an accompanying registered mailing) 5) posting (with or without an accompanying registered mailing) 6) any combination of #1-5 7) something completely different (by itself or in combination with any of #1-5).

The judge picks from among these options to devise a method of alternate service for the defendant. The method is designed to give the defendant *actual* notice of the divorce. But if the alternate service doesn't give actual notice, that's all right. Elusive and disappeared defendants are legally entitled to whatever notice alternate service provides, even if this means no actual notice.

When the defendant is elusive, the judge will probably order either mailing, tacking, household delivery or a combination of these. But these things won't work on disappeared defendants whose whereabouts are unknown. For them, judges normally order publication or posting. With either method, judges can order registered mailing of the service papers to the defendant's last known address. If that address appears to be outdated, the judge can skip the mailing and order publication or posting alone.

Whatever form alternate service takes, keep in mind that you cannot perform it yourself because you're disqualified from serving as a party to the divorce. Like regular service, you must have a server—a helper or professional server—to carry out alternate service. You can apply for and help with the alternate service, but the helper or server must serve the service papers for you (see "Preparing for Service" on page 68 for which papers make up your service papers).

Alternate Service for an Elusive Defendant

With an elusive defendant, you know his/her home and/or business address. Before you apply for alternate service, you must try service by delivery on the defendant at those or other places. For service by delivery, use the procedure described in "Service by Delivery" on page 72. Since the service will probably be difficult, use a professional server, such as a sheriff or commercial process server. Tell the server to attempt delivery not once but three or four times.

You must also ask the server to describe each attempt in the Verification of Process Server section of the Motion and Verification for Alternate Service (MC 303), which you should give to the server along with the service papers. The server's description of each delivery attempt must include specific information about the date, place and result of the attempt, as shown in the sample form at the end of this appendix.

If the server succeeds in serving the defendant during those attempts, you have obtained service on the defendant by delivery, and don't need alternate service. But if service by delivery fails, the server will return the service papers to you and you can apply for alternate service.

Make sure that the server has completed the Verification of Process Server section in the Motion and Verification for Alternate Service (MC 303), and then pay the server for the attempted service. You must complete the top portion of the Motion and Verification for Alternate Service (MC 303), above the verification section. Because you are trying to serve an elusive defendant, complete paragraph #2a of the motion showing that you know the defendant's current home and/or business address. You should also complete the caption and paragraph #1 of the Order for Alternate Service (MC 304), and return to the clerk with:

- Motion and Verification for Alternate Service   MC 303
  - original
  - one copy

- Order for Alternate Service   MC 304
  - original

- $20 motion fee

File the Motion and Verification for Alternate Service (MC 303) with the clerk. After filing, go to your judge's office and submit a copy of the Motion and Verification for Alternate Service (MC 303) and the original Order for Alternate Service (MC 304) to the judge's secretary. The judge will review your motion in his/her office (although probably not while you wait), so a court hearing on the motion won't be necessary. If the judge grants your motion for alternate service, get the papers back from the judge's office and make three photocopies of the Order for Alternate Service (MC 304). Return to the clerk and file the original.

Examine the Order for Alternate Service (MC 304) to see which method of alternate service the judge has designed for the defendant. It will probably be either mailing, tacking, household delivery or a combination of them. (If the judge has ordered several things, prepare multiple sets of the service papers and the Order for Alternate Service (MC 304) because you will need separate sets of these papers for each form of alternate service ordered.) However, the judge could order another method of alternate service, which would be described in paragraph #2d. If the judge orders publication or posting, see the sections on these below.

Mailing

For this type of mailing, ordinary first-class mailing is permissible. Have your helper or server mail the service papers and a copy of the Order for Alternate Service (MC 304) to the person named by the judge in paragraph #2a of the order. The recipient might be the defendant personally or a friend or relative of the defendant. The day of service is the day the mailing is sent, not received. After the mailing is sent, have the helper or server complete paragraph #1 in the Proof of Service section on the reverse of one of your copies of the Order for Alternate Service (MC 304).

Tacking

When tacking has been ordered, have your helper or server take the service papers and a copy of the Order for Alternate Service (MC 304) to the address indicated at paragraph #2b of the order, and attach them to the front door at this address. The day of service is the day the papers are tacked to the door. After tacking, the helper or server must complete paragraph #2 in the Proof of Service section on the reverse of the copy of the Order for Alternate Service (MC 304) that you're using to prove service.

Household Delivery

To use this service method, your helper or server takes the service papers and a copy of the Order for Alternate Service (MC 304) to the defendant's house and delivers them to any adult living there. The helper or server must also tell that person to give the papers to the defendant. The day of service is the day the papers are delivered to the person in defendant's household. After delivery, the helper or server must prove service on the reverse of your proof of service copy of the Order for Alternate Service (MC 304). In this case, proof of the household delivery is made in paragraph #3 in the Proof of Service section of that paper.

Proof of Service by Mailing, Tacking or Household Delivery

After service by mailing, tacking or household delivery has been proved on the reverse of a copy of the Order for Alternate Service (MC 304), make two copies of this paper and save one for filing later as your proof of service.

Alternate Service for a Disappeared Defendant

If you don't know the current home or business address of the defendant, you might be able to convince the court that the defendant has disappeared and obtain alternate service by publication or posting. But before you ask for that, you must prove the defendant's disappearance by searching for his/her current home and business addresses.

Your search will be shaped by the information you have about the defendant. If you don't know much, start with one of the general sources of information listed below, moving to specific sources as you find out more.

¶ *Telephone directory.*

- *Telephone books.* If you know the city where the defendant lives, look in the telephone book for that city. Many libraries keep large collections of telephone books.

- *CD-ROMs.* Libraries often have CD-ROMs with all the listed telephone numbers and addresses in the U.S. The two main ones are PhoneDisc and SelectPhone.

- *Internet search/telephone directories.* Many Web browsers have search functions, such as AOL's PeopleConnection, Yahoo's PeopleSearch or MSN's FindPeople. These are basically just compilations of all U.S. telephone directories (minus unlisted numbers). These Web browsers also offer more powerful searches for people, but at a steep price, which isn't always a good value.

  You can often find this same information at a telephone directory Web site, such as:
  - SwitchBoard.com
  - AnyWho.com
  - WhitePages.com

¶ *City/suburban directories* Libraries frequently have these "reverse" directories, such as Polk's and Bresser's, which cross-index names, addresses and telephone numbers in various ways (Polk: names, addresses and telephone numbers; Bresser: addresses and telephone numbers). So for example, if you have someone's telephone number, Polk's will give you that person's name and street address. Polk's is also online at www.mrpolk.com.

¶ *Internet search engine.* You can go to an Internet search engine, such as Google, AltaVista, AskJeeves or AlltheWeb, and type in the defendant's name. (If s/he has a common name, put the name inside quotation marks or you'll get too much unsorted information. Also, try variations in the first name.) Your search may reveal information about the defendant from newspaper articles, press releases, etc. Search via several search engines because they have different data.

¶ *News database.* The defendant may have been in the news recently. Check the Web site of the newspaper(s) in the defendant's area. Nexis (also available through Lexis) compiles a lot of this material. Nexis is expensive to subscribe to, but many libraries offer free access. Factiva is another service with similar data.

¶ *Motor vehicle records.* Like most states, Michigan provides information about licensed drivers and vehicle registration/ownership (title). This information isn't given as freely as it used to be (you once could get it over the telephone). Now you have to submit an application and have a good reason to receive the information.

In Michigan, driver's license and motor vehicle registration/ownership information is available from the Secretary of State's record lookup service. Call (517) 322-1624 and ask for a record lookup request form. Information is also available at www.michigan.gov/sos, under the "Services to Businesses" icon. In sec. 4D of the request form, say that you are making the request in connection with a civil proceeding. The fee for the request is $7.

In other states, these requests are typically handled by department of motor vehicles (DMV) offices. The Johnson and Knox book lists all these offices.

¶ *Voter registration.* If the defendant is registered to vote, you can obtain address information from the voting registrar, which is the city or township clerk in Michigan.

¶ *Real property records.* The defendant may have been involved in a real property transaction as a seller, buyer, mortgagor (mortgage-borrower), etc. You can get this information from:

• *County register of deeds.* At the register of deeds office there are indexes listing sellers or mortgagors (grantors) and buyers (grantees) of property. Some counties have put this information online; try the Web site of the county where you think the defendant's real property is located.

- Several private Internet companies provide real property information nationwide:

  Public Records Online at www.netronline.com/public_records.htm

  Search Systems at www.searchsystems.net

¶ *Association memberships.* If you know or believe the defendant belongs to a trade, professional or social organization, contact the organization for information.

- *Association directories.* These directories list associations which may have directories of members:

  Directories in Print, Detroit: Gale Group, 2004

  Encyclopedia of Associations, Detroit: Gale Group, 2004

  National Trade and Professional Associations of the United States, Buck Downs, et al., eds., Washington, DC: Columbia Books, 2004

- *State licensing bureau.* In Michigan, many trades and professions are regulated by the Bureau of Commercial Services. You can find out if someone is licensed to practice a trade or profession in the state by calling the bureau's licensing verification unit at (517) 241-9427, or go to www.michigan.gov/cis and select the "Online Services" icon.

¶ *School directories.* If the defendant is a student or faculty member at a school, get the school directory.

Has the defendant graduated from a school? Schools, especially colleges and universities, keep extensive data on their alumni. Contact the school directly for information or try www.alumni.net

¶ *Contact friends, relatives, etc.* Contact the defendant's friends, relatives, former neighbors, landlords and employers to see if they know where s/he is now.

¶ *Postal search.* The U.S. Postal Service discontinued the release of change-of-address information. But you can get the equivalent by:

1) Sending a first-class letter to the defendant's last known address. On the envelope, put your return address and just below that write: "Do not forward—Address correction requested"

2) If the defendant has an active change-of-address card on file (they last for one year), the letter will come back to you with the defendant's new address.

The defendant may have special characteristics or circumstances which will influence the search.

¶ *Military servicemember.* If the defendant is an active-duty servicemember, reservist, or veteran, there are special ways to search for the defendant. See "Divorcing a Defendant-Servicemember" on page 145 in Appendix D for more about locating active-duty servicemembers. The Johnson and Knox book on locating military personnel cited in that section also has tips on locating reservists and veterans.

¶ *Prisoner.* Do you know or suspect the defendant is an inmate at a state or federal prison? If you do, see "What If My Spouse or I Am Imprisoned?" on page 27 for more about finding prisoners through state and federal prison locator services.

¶ *Homeless person.* As transients, homeless people are naturally difficult to find. But the Salvation Army maintains a list, organized by region, of homeless people. You can request a search after paying a search fee. The Johnson and Knox book cited in this section lists the four regional centers; the Midwest center covering Michigan is:

> The Salvation Army
> Missing Persons Services
> 10 W. Algonquin Rd.
> Des Plaines, IL 60016
> (847) 294-2000

¶ *Overseas resident.* If the defendant is overseas, you may be able to find him/her through the U.S. Department of State:

1) Contact the state department's Passport Services Office and see if the defendant's passport contains an overseas destination and maybe even an address. Write the passport services at:

> Passport Services
> Research and Liaison Branch
> 111 19th St. NW
> Suite 200
> Washington, DC 20522

2) After you locate the country where the defendant is living, contact the U.S. embassy in that country. The embassy can often request the foreign country to provide the defendant's current address there. For help with these embassy requests, contact the U.S. Department of State at (202) 647-4000. Or you can try locating the defendant yourself in the foreign country using Infobel.com, an international telephone directory.

¶ *Professional search.* If you can afford it, hire a private investigator to find the defendant. They have access to special databases which are very effective. The cost is around $30-200 to do a basic search of five databases. For a PI in your area, look in the yellow pages or ask for a referral from:

Michigan Council of Private Investigators
(800) 266-6274
www.mcpihome.com

National Association of Investigative Specialists
(512) 719-3595
www.pimail.com/nais

During your search for the defendant, keep a written record of when and what you did. For example, if you contact relatives or friends of the defendant, record the date, person with whom you spoke and what s/he said. Keep any written evidence of your attempts to find the defendant, such as return-to-sender letters to him/her or correspondence with others about the defendant's disappearance. All this information is valuable because you will use it later when you apply for alternate service.

If you find the defendant's home and/or business address during your search, attempt service on him/her using one of the regular service methods.* But if you cannot locate the defendant, the failure will show that the defendant has disappeared, allowing you to apply for alternate service by publication or posting.

Complete the top portion of the Motion and Verification for Alternate Service (MC 303) above the Verification of Process Server section, which you can leave blank. Since you're trying to serve a disappeared defendant, complete paragraph #2b of the motion saying that you don't know the defendant's current home and business addresses.

After you complete the Motion and Verification for Alternate Service (MC 303), attach any written materials (undelivered letters, correspondence with the defendant's friends and relatives, etc.) showing that you failed to discover the defendant's whereabouts. Then complete the caption and first two lines of the Order for Service by Publication/Posting and Notice of Action (MC 307). After you prepare these papers, return to the clerk with:

- Motion and Verification for Alternate Service   MC 303
    - original
    - one copy

- Order for Service by Publication/Posting and Notice of
  Action   MC 307
    - original

- $20 motion fee

File the Motion and Verification for Alternate Service (MC 303) with the clerk. After filing, go to your judge's office and submit a copy of the Motion and Verification for Alternate Service (MC 303) and the original Order for Service by Publication/Posting and Notice of Action (MC 307) to the judge's

---

*   If you discover the defendant's current home or business address, but fail to have him/her served there, see above on serving an elusive defendant.

secretary. The judge will review your motion in his/her office (although probably not while you wait), so a court hearing on the motion won't be necessary. If the judge grants your motion for alternate service, get the papers back from the judge's office and make two photocopies of the Order for Service by Publication/Posting and Notice of Action (MC 307). Return to the clerk and file the original.

Examine the Order for Service by Publication/Posting and Notice of Action (MC 307) to see which method of alternate service the judge has devised for the defendant. It's probably either publication (paragraph #2) or posting (paragraph #3), and possibly a registered mailing (paragraph #4). If registered mailing has been ordered, make an extra photocopy of the Order for Service by Publication/Posting and Notice of Action (MC 307).

Publication

If the judge has ordered publication as the alternate service in your case, you must publish a legal advertisement in a newspaper. Maybe you have seen fine-print legal advertisements in your local newspaper. This is the kind of ad you must have published.

The court rules say that the legal advertisement must be published in a newspaper in the county where the defendant resides when you know the defendant's residence. If you don't know where the defendant is residing, the court rules permit advertisement in the county where the case is filed. Since your defendant has disappeared, you can advertise in the county where you filed for divorce, which is probably your county.

See which newspaper the judge has chosen as the publisher of your advertisement in paragraph #2 of the Order for Service by Publication/Posting and Notice of Action (MC 307). Take/send a copy of the MC 307 to that newspaper and ask it to prepare a legal advertisement for you. The newspaper will create an advertisement using the caption and paragraph #1 of the Order for Service by Publication/Posting and Notice of Action (MC 307). It will publish the advertisement as instructed in paragraph #2 of the order. Ordinarily, publication must be once a week for three consecutive weeks.

Once the advertisement has been published the required number of times, the newspaper will bill you for the cost of publication.* After you pay the bill, the newspaper will complete the Affidavit of Publishing on the

---

*   The cost of your advertisement depends on its size and the frequency of publication. Since you really only need to publish the caption and paragraph #1 of the Order for Service by Publication/Posting and Notice of Action (MC 307), your advertisement should not be very large. The newspaper may want to print the entire order, but that is unnecessary and will cost you more. Your advertisement will probably be published three times. In that case, there is a minimum charge of around $45, but the cost will probably be slightly more, perhaps $50-100.

reverse of the copy of the Order for Service by Publication/Posting and Notice of Action (MC 307) that you gave it and return this paper to you.

If the defendant's last known address is out of date, the judge will probably omit registered mailing of the service papers to the defendant. But if the defendant's last known address is fairly recent, registered mailing may be required.

If the judge has ordered registered mailing, have a helper mail the service papers and a copy of the Order for Service by Publication/Posting and Notice of Action (MC 307) to the defendant at his/her last known address. This mailing must be by registered (not certified) mail, return receipt requested. The mailing must be sent sometime before the date of the last publication of the legal advertisement.

Afterward, have your helper complete the Affidavit of Mailing on the reverse of a copy of the Order for Service by Publication/Posting and Notice of Action (MC 307), and attach both the Receipt for Registered Mail (PS Form 3806) and the Domestic Return Receipt (PS Form 3811), signed or unsigned by the defendant, to it. Your helper can use the Affidavit of Mailing on the same copy of the Order for Service by Publication/Posting and Notice of Action (MC 307) that the newspaper used to prove publication, or you can use another copy. Either way, make two copies of the reverse of the order(s) and save one for filing later as your proof of service.

Posting

Judges seem to prefer publication as the method of alternate service for disappeared defendants, and posting is seldom ordered. But if posting was ordered in your Order for Service by Publication/Posting and Notice of Action (MC 307), look at paragraph #3 to see who was designated as the poster. That person might be a sheriff, policeman or court official, such as a bailiff. Take four copies of the Order for Service by Publication/Posting and Notice of Action (MC 307) to the person designated as the poster and request posting of the order.

The poster will post the order in the courthouse and the two other public places the court has specified in paragraph #3. Ordinarily, the order will remain posted for three consecutive weeks. After the posting period expires, the poster will bill you for posting services and prove the posting in the Affidavit of Posting on the reverse of the extra copy of the Order for Service by Publication/Posting and Notice of Action (MC 307).

Like alternate service by publication, alternate service by posting can be with or without registered mailing of the service papers to the defendant. If the judge has ordered registered mailing in paragraph #4 of the Order for Service by Publication/Posting and Notice of Action (MC 307), have your helper mail the service papers and a copy of the MC 307 to the defendant at his/her last known address. This mailing should be made by registered (not certified) mail, return receipt requested. The mailing must be sent sometime before the last week of the posting.

Afterward, have your helper complete the Affidavit of Mailing on the reverse of a copy of the Order for Service by Publication/Posting and Notice of Action (MC 307), and attach both the Receipt for Registered Mail (PS Form

3806) and the Domestic Return Receipt (PS Form 3811), signed or unsigned by the defendant, to it. Your helper can complete the Affidavit of Mailing on the same copy of the Order for Service by Publication/Posting and Notice of Action (MC 307) that the poster used to prove posting, or you can use another copy. Either way, make two copies of the reverse of the order(s) and save one for filing later as your proof of service.

Original · Court
1st copy · Serving party
2nd copy · Extra

Approved, SCAO

STATE OF MICHIGAN
JUDICIAL DISTRICT
JUDICIAL CIRCUIT

MOTION AND VERIFICATION FOR ALTERNATE SERVICE

CASE NO.

Court telephone no.

Court address

Plaintiff name(s), address(es), and telephone number(s)

Defendant name(s), address(es), and telephone number(s)

v

1. Service of process upon _DUDLEY E. LOVELACE_ cannot reasonably be made as otherwise provided in MCR 2.105, as shown in the following verification of process server.

2. Defendant's last known home and business addresses are:
900 S. MAPLE _LAKE CITY_ _MI_ _48800_
Home address — City — State — Zip
1000 SERVICE RD.
Business address — City — State — Zip

a. I believe the ☒home ☒business address shown above is current.

b. I do not know defendant's current ☒home ☒business address. I have made the following efforts to ascertain the current address: _3-4-89 SEARCHED TELEPHONE AND CITY DIRECTORIES / 3-7-89 REQUESTED ADDRESS CORRECTION FROM USPS / 3-7-89 DID RECORD LOOKUP AT MICHIGAN SECRETARY OF STATE / 3-7-89 WROTE TO MABEL LOVELACE (MOTHER) (SEE ATTACHED LETTER); ALL WITHOUT RESULTS._

3. I request the court order service by alternate means.

I declare that the statements above are true to the best of my information, knowledge and belief.

Darlene A. Lovelace
Attorney signature — Bar no.

_3-15-89_
Date

Attorney name (type or print)

Address

Telephone no.

City, state, zip

VERIFICATION OF PROCESS SERVER

1. I have tried to serve process on this defendant as described: State date, place, and what occurred on each occasion

3-4-89 TRIED TO SERVE DEFENDANT AT 900 S. MAPLE, LAKE CITY, MI, BUT A WOMAN THERE TOLD ME DEFENDANT WAS NOT AT HOME WHEN IT APPEARED HE WAS.

3-5-89 " TRIED TO SERVE DEFENDANT AT 1000 SERVICE RD, LAKE CITY, MI,
3-7-89 " BUT HIS EMPLOYER PREVENTED SERVICE.
3-8-89 TRIED TO SERVE DEFENDANT AT 1000 SERVICE RD, LAKE CITY, MI, BUT HE SPED AWAY IN HIS CAR.

I declare that the statements above are true to the best of my information, knowledge and belief.

Chester Gunn
Signature
CHESTER GUNN
Process Server (type or print)

_3-14-89_
Date

MCR 2.105

...TION FOR ALTERNATE SERVICE

COMPLETE 2b. INSTEAD FOR A _DISAPPEARED_ DEFENDANT

COMPLETE 2a. FOR AN _ELUSIVE_ DEFENDANT

SERVER MUST COMPLETE VERIFICATION OF PROCESS SERVER FOR ATTEMPTED SERVICE ON AN _ELUSIVE_ DEFENDANT

Approved, SCAO

STATE OF MICHIGAN JUDICIAL DISTRICT JUDICIAL CIRCUIT	ORDER FOR ALTERNATE SERVICE	Original - Court 1st copy - Defendant 2nd copy - Plaintiff 3rd copy - Return

Court address

Plaintiff name(s), address(es), and telephone no.(s)	Court telephone no.
	Defendant name(s), address(es), and telephone no.(s)
Plaintiff's attorney, bar no., address, and telephone no.	

v

THE COURT FINDS:

1. Service of process upon defendant ___DUDLEY E. LOVELACE___

cannot reasonably be made as provided in MCR 2.105, and service of process may be made in a manner which is reasonably calculated to give defendant actual notice of the proceedings and an opportunity to be heard.

IT IS ORDERED:

2. Service of the summons and complaint and a copy of this order may be made by the following method(s):

  a. ☒ First class mail to ___900 S. MAPLE, LAKE CITY, MI___

  b. ☒ Tacking or firmly affixing to the door at _____ "

  c. ☒ Delivering at _____

      to a member of defendant's household who is of suitable age and discretion to receive process, with instructions to deliver it promptly to defendant.

  d. ☐ Other: _____

JUDGE WILL CHOOSE ONE OR MORE OF THESE METHODS

3. For each method used, proof of service must be filed promptly with the court.

___3-17-89___
Date

___Lester Jubbs___
Judge

Bar no.

MC 304 (3/00) ORDER FOR ALTERNATE SERVICE

MCR 2.103, MCR 2.105

PROOF OF SERVICE

I served a copy of the summons and complaint and a copy of the order for alternate service upon _____ by:

DUDLEY E. LOVELACE   on SAT. 3-18-89
                                                                              Date

1. First class mail to   900 S. MAPLE, LAKE CITY, MI   , on SAT. 3-18-89
                                                                              Date

2. Tacking or firmly affixing to the door at _____ "_____ , on MON. 3-20-89
                                                                              Date

3. Delivering at _____ suitable age and discretion to receive process, with instructions to deliver

   to a member of _____

   it promptly to defen _____   , on _____
                                                                              Date

4. Other: _____

                                                          Ruth Darling
                                                          Signature

3-21-89
Date

| Service fee | Miles traveled | Mileage fee | Total fee | Title
|-------------|----------------|-------------|-----------|
| $ | | $ | $ |

                                                          OJIBWAY   County, Michigan.

Subscribed and sworn to before me on 3-21-89
                                        Date

My commission expires: 1-1-90   Signature: Loretta Smiley
                        Date   Deputy court clerk/Notary public

Speech bubble: DAY OF SERVICE

Speech bubble: HELPER/SERVER MUST PROVE EVERY SERVICE METHOD ORDERED AND USED

Speech bubble: IF SEVERAL SERVICE METHODS WERE USED ON DIFFERENT DAYS, USE LAST DAY AS DAY OF SERVICE (3-20-89 IN THIS CASE)

Appendix C: Obtaining Alimony

If you and the defendant have agreed on the payment of periodic alimony, you must take several extra steps described in this appendix. At the beginning of your divorce, you must ask for alimony in paragraph #8c of your Complaint for Divorce (GRP 1),* and then show: 1) your need for the alimony 2) the defendant's ability to pay it. If you omit this request, you may not be able to get alimony later.

Alimony and the Friend of the Court

The friend of the court is a family court official with a number of duties in divorce cases. In with-children cases, the friend of the court investigates and makes recommendations to the judge about divorce issues, referees and mediates disputes, reviews, modifies and enforces orders. The friend of the court used to collect and distribute support, but these duties have been transferred to a new financial agency in Lansing, the state disbursement unit (SDU).

The friend of the court isn't normally involved in divorce cases without minor children. However, the friend of the court is supposed to take part in no-children cases whenever alimony is sought. Despite this rule, these days the friend of the court doesn't always participate in alimony cases, thanks to a law passed in 2002.

---

*   As mentioned in "Alimony" on page 11, the divorce papers call alimony by its real name: spousal support.

Friend of the Court: In or Out of Your Divorce Case?

According to the new law, it's now possible to "opt out" of the friend of the court system. After opting out, the friend of the court never enters the case (for an opt-out from a new case) or withdraws from the case and closes its file (after an opt-out from an open case).

Is an opt-out worth considering? If your divorce is amicable with a willing and reliable alimony-payer, it may make sense. But don't underestimate the value of the friend of the court when alimony or other support is at stake. The friend of the court performs an important bookkeeping function, keeping track of support payments. Without a neutral third party like the friend of the court, it's one party's word against the other when a dispute breaks out. In this way a dispute over alimony can escalate, turning an amicable divorce into a bitter one.

Staying in the Friend of the Court System

If you want to remain in the friend of the court system, add the friend of the court to your case by taking the following extra steps:

Notice to the friend of the court. The friend of the court must receive notice of your divorce by getting copies of all your divorce papers. To do that, make extra copies of the divorce papers (generally three instead of two) and mark the upper left corners of the copies with the notation "FOC." As you file your divorce papers with the clerk, give the extra marked copies to the clerk. The clerk will forward these to the friend of the court.

Information for the friend of the court. Although the divorce papers provide a good deal of information about your marriage, the friend of the court needs more personal and financial information. The friend of the court gets that extra information in the Verified Statement (FOC 23). This paper must be given to the clerk along with your initial divorce papers when you file for divorce. Unlike the other divorce papers, the clerk doesn't place the Verified Statement (FOC 23) in your court file. Instead, the clerk forwards the statement to the friend of the court, without keeping a copy for itself. However, a copy of the Verified Statement (FOC 23) must be included in your service papers and served on the defendant.

Friend of the court fee. You must pay a special fee to cover the cost of the friend of the court's services in your case.* The amount of the fee varies according to the friend of the court's involvement in a divorce:
- $30 in cases with no investigation or mediation by the friend of the court
- $50 in cases mediated by the friend of the court

---

*   You may be excused from paying the friend of the court fee if you
      obtain a fee exemption, as described in Appendix A.

- $70 in cases where there is an investigation and recommendation by the friend of the court

You will probably owe the minimum $30 fee since neither mediation nor investigation/recommendation should be necessary when alimony is uncontested. The law seems to require payment of the friend of the court at the end of the divorce. But some counties want the fee up front, at filing.

Friend of the court pamphlet. While you're at the clerk's office filing your divorce, ask the clerk for two copies of the friend of the court pamphlet. The pamphlet describes the office of the friend of the court and its role in divorce. Keep one pamphlet for yourself. The other must be served on the defendant with the service papers. After service, list the friend of the court pamphlet in the proof of service as having been served on the defendant.

Because you aren't contesting alimony, the friend of the court probably won't intervene in your divorce. But it could decide to investigate alimony and submit a recommendation to the judge on the issue. If so, you should take the recommendation into account when you prepare the alimony provision in your divorce judgment. Whatever happens, see "Alimony Provisions" in Appendix F for more about providing for either short- or long-term alimony in your judgment.

Opting Out of the Friend of the Court System

Opting out of the friend of the court system takes more than just notifying the friend of the court. There are in fact three types of opt-outs. And there are several restrictions on opting out, and automatic triggers for bringing cases back under friend of the court control.

Types of Opt-Outs

The 2002 opt-out law allows several kinds of opt-outs from the friend of the court system:

- total opt-out from all friend of the court services
- partial opt-out from all friend of the court services except collection and distribution of support through the state disbursement unit (SDU) (with or without immediate income withholding as the method of payment)
- limited opt-out from immediate income withholding only, but receipt of all other friend of the court services

Total Opt-Out

In some cases, you can opt out of the friend of the court system completely, giving up all friend of the court services in your divorce. Afterward, you are responsible for all future management of your case, including payment of alimony (you lose SDU-payment of alimony with a total opt-out). You must have the consent of the defendant to get (and keep) a total opt-out. And the judge must review and approve your opt-out request.

The timing of an opt-out is important. You can get a total opt-out at the beginning of a divorce (new case) or later while the case is pending (open case). The procedures for new- and open-case opt-outs are a little different, and these are described below.

Total Opt-Out in a New Case

You can opt out of a new-filed case, so the friend of the court never enters the case and never opens a file for the case. Not every case is eligible for this kind of opt-out. The opt-out law bars opting out of a new case when:

- a party is eligible for FIA services (also known as title IV-D services) because of past or current receipt of public assistance
- a party is applying for FIA services
- a party requests friend of the court services
- there is evidence of 1) domestic violence, or 2) uneven bargaining position between the parties, and evidence that a party hasn't applied for FIA services against the best interests of that party or any children

If your case is eligible for opting out, you must request an opt-out at the start of your divorce, when you file. As you prepare your initial divorce papers (see "Filing" on page 61 for more about preparing these papers), make additions to one of these papers:

- Complaint for Divorce (GRP 1), in paragraph #8d check the "other relief" box, and then in the blank space insert: "I request an opt-out from all friend of the court services" (total opt-out)

You must also prepare three extra papers, which will be referred to as the "opt-out papers:

- Advice of Rights Regarding Use of Friend of the Court Services   FOC 101   2

- Supplemental Notice to Advice of Rights Regarding Use of Friend of the Court Services   FOC 101a   2

- Order Exempting Case from Friend of the Court Services   FOC   2

The FOC 101 and 101a warn you which services you lose by opting out. You and the defendant must receive separate copies of these forms, and both of you must date and sign the original forms, which will be filed with court. This tells the court that both parties consent to the opt-out.

The FOC 102 is the actual opt-out order. You select a total opt-out by leaving both boxes in paragraph #13a and b unchecked. The sample form shows you how to do this. Afterward, paperclip the signed FOC 101 and 101a to the FOC 102.

After you file your divorce, you must bring the opt-out request to the judge right away. By acting quickly, you can keep the friend of the court out of the case before it opens a file. The best way is to take your (unfiled) opt-out papers to the judge's office and ask the judge's secretary or law clerk to pass these onto the judge for review.

If the judge approves an opt-out, file the opt-out papers with the clerk (the friend of the court won't get copies since it has dropped out of the case), and serve another set of copies on the defendant with the service papers (see "Service" on page 67 for more about service). After receiving a denial, you must withdraw you opt-out papers and the judge will note the denial on the Complaint for Divorce (GRP 1) or in the case file.

After an opt-out, the friend of the court won't participate in your case. As a result, skip all the extra steps and papers, such as the Verified Statement (FOC 23), described in "Staying in the Friend of the Court System" above.

As the divorce continues, you may change your mind and want the friend of the court back in your case. All you have to do is submit a simple written request to the friend of the court; no motion is necessary. You can use the Request to Reopen Friend of the Court Case (FOC 104) for this purpose. The friend of the court will also intervene on its own when: 1) either party requests friend of the court services 2) a party applies for public assistance.

At the end of the divorce, you must decide whether you want the friend of the court in or out of your case during the post-divorce (called the post-judgment) period. During this time, which lasts until the alimony terminates, the friend of the court provides services for modification and enforcement of the divorce judgment (the FOC 101 has a good summary of these post-judgment duties).

If you still want the friend of the court out of the case, you must say so in the Judgment of Divorce (GRP 4). Ordinarily, the opt-out order would expire according to paragraph #10 of the Judgment of Divorce (GRP 4a), as a nonfinal order. But you can extend the opt-out order in paragraph #16a of the Judgment of Divorce (GRP 4x). Check the outdented paragraph box and then the first box inside the paragraph to opt out again from all friend of the court services (total opt-out).

Since you're having the alimony paid from payer directly to payee, without immediate income withholding through the SDU, you must provide for this in paragraph #14 of the Judgment of Divorce (GRP 4x). Check the correct boxes in paragraph #14. Omit the Income Withholding Order (FOC 5) from your final divorce papers, because this is unnecessary. Also, describe the opt-out to the judge during your testimony at the final hearing.

If you want the friend of the court back in your case post-judgment, you could file a Request to Reopen Friend of the Court Case (FOC 104) before the hearing. Or you can do nothing and let the FOC 102 expire as a nonfinal order according to paragraph #10 of the Judgment of Divorce (GRP 4a). Don't forget to select the correct method of alimony payment in paragraph #14 of the GRP 4x, adding the FOC 5 if needed.

There's yet another choice: You want to change the opt-out, switching from a total opt-out to a partial or limited one. For a partial opt-out, see "Partial Opt-Out" for general information and "Partial Opt-Out in an Open Case" below about the steps for opting out at the end of a divorce. Likewise, see "Limited Opt-Out" and "Limited Opt-Out in an Open Case" below about limited opt-outs.

To switch opt-outs, let the previous opt-out order expire as a nonfinal order, as described above. Then in paragraph #16a of the GRP 4x, choose the new opt-out you want by checking the second box (for a partial opt-out) or the third box (for a limited one) inside that paragraph. Also, explain the switch to the judge at the final hearing.

Total Opt-Out in an Open Case

The friend of the court may have participated in your case while it was pending. But now you want to opt out totally from the friend of the court system for the post-divorce (called the post-judgment) period. It's possible to have the friend of the court withdraw from the case and close its file that way with the consent of the defendant and approval of the court.

Not every open divorce case is eligible for total opt out. Like a new case, there are several restrictions which are similar but not the same as the ones for a new case:

- a party objects to opting out
- a party is eligible to receive FIA services (also known as title IV-D services) because the party receives public assistance
- a party is eligible to receive FIA services because the party received public assistance and an arrearage is owed to the state
- no support arrearage or custody or parenting time order violation (for cases with children) has occurred in the last 12 months
- neither party has reopened a friend of the court case during the last 12 months
- there is evidence of 1) domestic violence, or 2) uneven bargaining position between the parties, and evidence that a party is opting out against the best interests of that party or any children

If you want to opt out late in your case, the final hearing, when the divorce judgment is granted, is a convenient time. Otherwise, you must file a separate motion and schedule a hearing on your request. Before the final hearing, prepare three extra "opt-out papers:"

- Advice of Rights Regarding Use of   FOC 101   2
  Friend of the Court Services

- Supplemental Notice to Advice of Rights   FOC 101a   2
  Regarding Use of Friend of the Court Ser-
  vices

- Order Exempting Case from Friend of the   FOC   2
  Court Services

The FOC 101 and 101a warn you which services you lose by opting out. You and the defendant must receive separate copies of these forms, and both of you must date and sign the original forms which will be filed with the court. This tells the court that both parties consent to the opt-out.

The FOC 102 is the actual opt-out order. You select a total opt-out by leaving both boxes in paragraph #13a and b unchecked. The sample form shows you how to make the correct choice. Afterward, paperclip the signed FOC 101 and 101a to the FOC 102.

You must also prepare your Judgment of Divorce (GRP 4) to provide for a total opt-out. In paragraph #16a of the Judgment of Divorce (GPR 4x), check the outdented paragraph box to show that you are opting out. And then inside that paragraph, check the first box opting out of "all friend of the court services." In paragraph #14, choose your new method of alimony payment, without income withholding and probably with payment directly to the payee. Also, omit the Income Withholding Order (FOC 5) from your final divorce papers.

During the final hearing, include the FOC 101, 101a and 102 among your final divorce papers (see "Final Hearing" on page 87 for more about preparing, filing and sending the final divorce papers to the defendant after the divorce). In your testimony, say that you want to opt out. It's also helpful to have the defendant on hand to confirm the opt-out; but the defendant's signing the FOC 101 and 101a is sufficient to show consent.

If the judge denies your opt-out request, just correct the Judgment of Divorce (GRP 4) by removing all the opt-out provisions described above, and choose payment of alimony by immediate income withholding to the SDU in paragraph #14 of the GRP 4x.

After opting out, the friend of the court won't help with any judgment modification or enforcement during the post-judgment period. But if you want the friend of the court back in, just file the Request to Reopen Friend of the Court Case (FOC 104). The friend of the court will also re-enter the case automatically if: 1) either party requests friend of the court services 2) a party applies for public assistance.

Partial Opt-Out

Ordinarily, when you opt-out totally from the friend of the court system you give up all friend of the court services, including payment of alimony through the SDU. SDU-payment is an efficient means of collecting and distributing support, and not everyone opting out wants to lose this.

Luckily, the 2002 opt-out law allows partial opt-outs: You give up all friend of the court services except payment of alimony to the SDU. If you choose this option, you also have two subchoices: 1) SDU-payment by immediate income withholding 2) SDU-payment without immediate income withholding, and payment from the payer directly to the SDU.

A partial opt-out is a lot like a total opt-out (they're really just different choices on the Order Exempting Case from Friend of the Court Services (FOC 102), and they share similar procedures. And as with a total opt-out, you can opt out partially from a new case (before the friend of the court's entry into the case) or an open case (after the FOC has entered the case). However, new-case partial opt-outs aren't dealt with because they primarily concern payment of temporary alimony, which this book doesn't provide for (see "Do I Need 'Preliminary Relief?'" on page 37 for more about temporary alimony).

Partial Opt-Out in an Open Case

Partially opting out from an open case resembles an open-case total opt-out. And the same six restrictions (objection, eligibility for FIA services, etc.) apply. See "Total Opt-Out in an Open Case" above for more about these procedures and restrictions.

There is a difference in the paperwork. When you prepare the FOC 102, pay close attention to paragraph #13 (unused in a total opt-out). This is where a partial opt-out occurs. Having opted out of the friend of the court system, you, in essence, opt back in for SDU-payment.

After you opt back for SDU collection, you have a choice: Do you want the SDU to collect the alimony by immediate income withholding or by direct payment from the payer? By checking #13a, you get SDU-payment by immediate income withholding. You have to set up the withholding yourself (or continue it), the friend of the court won't do this for you. With choice #13b, you elect payment from the payer to the SDU, without immediate income withholding.

> **More Information**
>
> About paying support to the state disbursement unit (SDU), call the unit at (866) 540-0008 or use its Web site: www.mi-sdu.com.

Your Judgment of Divorce must also mirror the choices you have made. In paragraph #14, you want to check payment to the SDU. But in the line above, choose the immediate income withholding box for payment by income withholding (matches #13a on the FOC 102) or no income withholding (matches #13b on the FOC 102) for direct payment to the SDU. If you skip immediate income withholding, omit the FOC 5 from your final divorce papers.

Limited Opt-Out

You may be comfortable with the friend of the court's management of your case; all you want is a different method of alimony payment. The law allows you to opt out of immediate income withholding only, which is the normal means of paying alimony, and choose another payment method. Other payment options include: 1) payment to the SDU directly 2) direct payment to the alimony payee/recipient.

After a limited opt-out, you will have access to the usual friend of the court services. You may or may not have SDU collection and distribution of support. But either way, the friend of the court will monitor payments and enforce the alimony order.

There are two ways to avoid immediate income withholding through a limited opt-out: 1) with the consent of the defendant 2) for "good cause," without the consent of the defendant. Either kind requires court approval.

As with total and partial opt-outs, there is a restriction on limited opt-outs. You can't opt for good cause if alimony is already past due. And like other types of opt-outs, you can get a limited opt-out from a new case or an open case. New-case limited opt-outs are omitted here becase they concern payment of temporary alimony, which this book lacks.

Limited Opt-Out in an Open Case

The final hearing is a good time to ask for a limited opt-out because you're going before the judge anyway. Prior to the final hearing, prepare one or two extra "opt-out papers." To opt out with the agreement of the defendant, you need both forms; opt-outs for cause use the order only:

- Agreement Suspending Immediate Income Withholding   FOC 63   3

- Order Suspending Immediate Income Withholding   FOC 64   3

You must obtain the consent of the defendant for an agreed-to opt-out. At a minimum, the defendant must sign the FOC 63. It's also helpful if the defendant can attend the final hearing and confirm that s/he agrees to alimony payment without immediate income withholding. But the defendant's signing the FOC 63 should be sufficient to show consent.

You must also prepare your Judgment of Divorce (GRP 4x) to account for the opt-out. In paragraph # 16, check the outdented box and the last box inside the first paragraph indicating that the opt-out is from immediate income withholding only. In paragraph #14, check the second box showing that alimony isn't being paid by immediate income withholding, and choose payment to either the SDU or the payee. Also, omit the Income Withholding Order (FOC 5), since this goes with immediate income withholding.

During the final hearing, include the FOC 63 and/or 64 among your final divorce papers (see "Final Hearing" on page 87 for more about preparing, filing and sending final divorce papers to the defendant). In your testimony, say that you want to avoid immediate income withholding and describe your alternate method of payment.

If the judge denies your opt-out request, just correct the Judgment of Divorce (GRP 4x) to provide for immediate income withholding and add back the FOC 5.

If the judge approves your opt-out request, the alimony will be paid without immediate income withholding. If you want it back, you must file a motion. The friend of the court will also take steps to reimpose immediate income withholding when past-due alimony equals or exceeds one month of support.

	Original - Friend of the Court 1st copy - Plaintiff/Attorney 2nd copy - Defendant/Attorney

Approved, SCAO

STATE OF MICHIGAN JUDICIAL CIRCUIT COUNTY	VERIFIED STATEMENT	CASE NO.

1. Mother's last name LOVELACE	First name DARLENE	Middle name ANN	2. Any other names by which wife is or has been known	
3. Date of birth 5-1-65		4. Social security number 380-16-1010	5. Driver license number and state M 650 603 440 886 MICH.	

6. Mailing address and residence address (if different)
121 S. MAIN, LAKE CITY, MI 48800

7. Eye color BLUE	8. Hair color BLONDE	9. Height 5'6"	10. Weight 120	11. Race WHITE	12. Scars, tattoos, etc.	
13. Home telephone no. 772-0000	14. Work telephone no. 772-0011			15. Maiden name ALBRIGHT	16. Occupation WAITRESS	18. Gross weekly income $250

17. Business/Employer's name and address
10,000 PANCAKES, 111 M-78, LAKE CITY, MI 48800

19. Has wife applied for or does she receive public assistance? If yes, please specify kind. ☐ Yes ☒ No	20. AFDC and recipient identification numbers

21. Father's last name LOVELACE	First name DUDLEY	Middle name ERNEST	22. Any other names by which husband is or has been known	
23. Date of birth 6-15-64		24. Social security number 379-10-5567	25. Driver license number and state M 649 601 402 701 MICH.	

26. Mailing address and residence address (if different)
900 S. MAPLE, LAKE CITY, MI 48800

27. Eye color BROWN	28. Hair color BLACK	29. Height 6'	30. Weight 170	31. Race WHITE	32. Scars, tattoos, etc.	
33. Home telephone no. 773-3004	34. Work telephone no. 773-0011			35. Occupation SALESMAN		37. Gross weekly income $375

36. Business/Employer's name and address
WATERBED WORLD, 1000 SERVICE RD., LAKE CITY, MI 48800

38. Has husband applied for or does he receive public assistance? If yes, please specify kind. ☐ Yes ☒ No	39. AFDC and recipient identification numbers

40. a. Name of Minor Child Involved in Case	b. Birth Date	c. Age	d. Soc. Sec. No.	e. Residential Address

41. a. Name of Other Minor Child of Either Party	b. Birth Date	c. Age	d. Soc. Sec. No.	e. Residential Address

42. Health care coverage available for each minor child a. Name of Minor Child	b. Name of Policy Holder	c. Name of Insurance Co./HMO	d. Policy/Certificate/Contract No.

43. Names and addresses of person(s) other than parties, if any, who may have custody of child(ren) during pendency of this case

• If any of the public assistance information above changes before your judgment is entered, you are required to give the Friend of the Court written notice of the change.

I declare that the statements above are true to the best of my information, knowledge, and belief.

Darlene A. Lovelace
Signature

2-28-89
Date

FOC 23 (5/93) VERIFIED STATEMENT

MCR 3.206(B)

Approved, SCAO

STATE OF MIC...
JUDIC...

Friend of the Court addre...

1. Right to Refuse F...

a. You have the rig...
court involvement...
services not be r...
provided both pa...

1) Neither of y...
2) There is no...
3) The court fir...

b. If you already ha...
parties agree, a...

1) Neither of y...
2) There is no...
3) The court fi...
4) No money i...
5) No arrearag...
6) Neither of y...

2. Friend of the Cou...

The friend of the co...
you choose to refu...

a. **Accounting Se...**

Friends of the ...
1) friend of the ...
and 3) annual s...

b. **Support Enfor...**

The friend of th...
child support e...

• Paying supp...
• Asking the ...
• Having unpa...
• Reporting s...
• Collecting s...

If you choose r...
of the court is ...
changing inc...

c. **Medical Supp...**

The friend of t...
the amounts t...
authorized to ...

d. **Support Revi...**

Once every tw...
After completi...
recommends ...
modified.

FOC 101 (6/03) AD...

Advice of Rights Rega...

e. **Custody and Pare...**

For friend of the c...
it is violated. Child...

• Asking the cour...
order.
• Suspending the...
• Awarding make...
• Joint meetings...

f. **Custody and Pa...**

For disputes abou...
and provide repo...

g. **Mediation Servi...**

Friend of the cou...
parenting time di...

3. State Disbursemen...

a. **State Disburser...**

If you choose no...
through, the stat...
cannot provide y...

All payments ma...
more than one c...
**friend of the co...
in the same ma...
to use the SDU...**

b. **Your Rights U...**

Title IV-D of the...
funding to be us...
of the court. If ...

**Check below only i...
must be attached t...**

I have read this advi...

☒ I acknowledge th...
this choice can ta...
approval. I also ...
rights.

Dar/en...
Signature

If you did not che...
court services, yo...

I request IV-D serv...

Date

Original - Court (to be filed with motion)

... continued from page 1

Approved, SCAO

STATE OF MICHIGAN JUDICIAL CIRCUIT COUNTY	SUPPLEMENTAL NOTICE TO ADVICE OF RIGHTS REGARDING USE OF FRIEND OF THE COURT SERVICES	Original - Court (to be filed with motion) 1st copy - Plaintiff 2nd copy - Defendant

Friend of the Court address

CASE NO.

Telephone no.

1. State Disbursement Unit Payments

a. **State Disbursement Unit (SDU)**

If you opt out of the friend of the court, you may continue to make payments through the State Disbursement Unit (SDU). The SDU uses the friend of the court for most accounting functions and cannot provide you with all of the accounting functions the friend of the court provides.

For friend of the court cases, payments are made through the SDU and distributed to the amounts due as required by federal law. When a payer has more than one case, federal law determines how a payment is divided between the cases. Even if parties opt out of the friend of the court, payments through the SDU must be divided between all payer's cases and distributed in the same manner as payments on friend of the court cases.

b. **SDU Limitations**

The SDU relies on the friend of the court records to determine the amount of income withholding. The SDU also requires the friend of the court to set up any income withholding or change in income withholding. If you choose not to accept friend of the court services, the SDU will not be able to process payments through income withholding if the person paying support changes jobs or the amount withheld changes.

Under federal law, the state of Michigan is converting its friend of the court to a new single child support enforcement computer system. County friend of the court offices will be converted under a schedule that begins in March, 2003 and continues until September 30, 2003. Until the conversion is completed, only the friend of the court can process checks. If you choose not to accept friend of the court services, you will not be able to use the SDU until all of your cases are converted to MiCSES version 2.4 or greater.

2. Your Acknowledgment of System Limitations on Your Right to Opt Out of Friend of the Court Services

Please sign and return this form to the friend of the court.

I have read this form and I want to opt out of the friend of the court. I understand that I cannot opt out of the friend of the court with SDU services until this case is converted to MiCSES version 2.4 or greater.

2-28-89
Date

Darlene Lovelace
Signature

Dudley Lovelace

DATE: 2-28-89

FOC 101a (6/03) SUPPLEMENTAL NOTICE TO ADVICE OF RIGHTS REGARDING USE OF FRIEND OF THE COURT SERVICES

Approved, SCAO

STATE OF MICHIGAN	Original - Court	
JUDICIAL CIRCUIT	1st copy - Plaintiff	
COUNTY	ORDER EXEMPTING CASE FROM FRIEND OF THE COURT SERVICES	2nd copy - Defendant 3rd copy - Friend of the Court

Friend of the Court address

CASE NO.

Plaintiff's name and address

FAX no.   Telephone no.

Defendant's name and address

v

Attorney:

Attorney:

Date of hearing: 3-1-89

Bar no.

THE COURT FINDS:
1. There is no evidence of domestic
2. Granting the parties the relief the
3. The parties have filed execut
4. Neither party receives publi
5. No money is due the state
6. No arrearage or custody
7. Neither party has reopen
☒ 8. The parties do not wa
   checked unless exceptional

between the parties to the case.
interests of any child in the case.
will not receive if their motion is granted.

IT IS ORDERED:
9. Subject to the provisions
☒ 10. This case is not a title
11. The friend of the court shal
   time, or support in this case.
12. The parties are responsible for a
13. Except as indicated below, there is n
   and the friend of the court shall terminate a
   the payer must keep the friend of the court
   care coverage that is available to the paye
   insurance company, health care organiz
   and the names and birth dates of the p
   ☐ a. Support shall be paid through th
      extent allowed by statutes and court rules
      The friend of the court shall notify the employer that it is no longer involved in the case and that any further information
      concerning income withholding will be provided by the parties.
   ☐ b. Support shall be paid through the SDU.
      If support payments are to be made through the SDU by income withholding or otherwise, the friend of the court shall not close
      the friend of the court case until the SDU notifies the friend of the court that it has been provided with the information necessary
      to process the child support payments. There will be no accounting for support that is not paid through the SDU.
14. The friend of the court shall open a friend of the court case if a party applies for public assistance relating to a child of the parties
   or either party submits to the friend of the court a written request to reopen the friend of the court case. If this case becomes
   a friend of the court case for any reason, the provisions on the other side of this order shall apply.

months in this case.

be closed. (Note: This box should be

unting functions for custody, parenting

ody, parenting time, or support in this case.
will be paid directly by the payer to the payee,
Should this case become a friend of the court case,
the name and address of the payer's source of income and any health
benefit of employment or that the payer maintains including the name of the
or health maintenance organization; the policy, certificate, or contract number;
ns for whose benefit the payer maintains the coverage.
State Disbursement Unit (SDU). Support shall be paid by income withholding to the

3-1-89
Date

See provisions on back.

Lester Jubbs
Judge

CERTIFICATE OF MAILING

I certify that on this date I mailed a copy of this order to the other party by ordinary mail addressed to the last known address.

Date

Signature

FOC 102 (6/03) ORDER EXEMPTING CASE FROM FRIEND OF THE COURT SERVICES

MCL 552.505, MCL 552.505a

Original - Court
1st copy - Friend of the Court

2nd copy - Plaintiff
3rd copy - Defendant

Approved, SCAO

STATE OF MICHIGAN
JUDICIAL CIRCUIT
COUNTY

REQUEST TO REOPEN
FRIEND OF THE COURT CASE

CASE NO.

Telephone no.

Friend of the Court address

Defendant's name and address

Plaintiff's name and address

Attorney:

Attorney:

1. On **3-1-89** an order was entered exempting this case from friend of the court services.
Date

I REQUEST that the friend of the court case be reopened upon filing of this request with the friend of the court office.

CERTIFICATE OF MAILING

I certify that on this date I mailed a copy of this request to the other party by ordinary mail addressed to the last known address.

Darlene Lovelace
Signature

4-1-89
Date

MCL 552.505, MCL 552.505a

FOC 104 (6/03) **REQUEST TO REOPEN FRIEND OF THE COURT CASE**

Original - Court
2nd copy - Friend of the Court
3rd copy - Plaintiff
4th copy - Defendant

CASE NO.

Approved, SCAO

| STATE OF MICHIGAN JUDICIAL CIRCUIT COUNTY | AGREEMENT SUSPENDING IMMEDIATE INCOME WITHHOLDING | |

Court telephone no.

Friend of the Court address

Plaintiff's name and address

NOTE: MCL 552.604(3); MSA 25.164(4)(3) requires that all new and modified support orders after December 31, 1990 include a provision for immediate income withholding and that income withholding take effect immediately unless the parties enter into a written agreement that the income withholding order shall not take effect immediately.

v

Defendant's name and address

We understand that by law an order of income withholding in a support order shall take ef~~~ agree to the following:

1. The order of income withholding shall not take effect immediately.

2. An alternative payment arrangement shall be made as follows:

DESCRIBE OTHER METHOD OF PAYMENT

THE DEFENDANT SHALL PAY THE SUPPORT DIREGLY TO THE SDU.

3. Both the payer and the recipient of support shall keep the friend of the court informed of the following:
   a. the name, address, and telephone number of his/her current source of income;
   b. any health care coverage that is available to him/her as a benefit of employment or that is maintained by him/her; the name of the insurance company, health care organization, or health maintenance organization; the policy, certificate or contract number; and the name(s) and birth date(s) of the person(s) for whose benefit s/he maintains health care coverage under the policy, certificate, or contract; and
   c. his/her current residence and mailing address.

4. We further understand that proceedings to implement income withholding shall commence if the payer of support falls one month behind in his/her support payments.

5. We recognize that the court may order withholding of income to take effect immediately for cause or at the request of the payer.

5-5-89
Date
Darlene Lovelace
Plaintiff's signature

5-5-89
Date
Dudley Lovelace
Defendant's signature

MCL 552.604; MSA 25.164(4)

FOC 63 (4/01) AGREEMENT SUSPENDING IMMEDIATE INCOME WITHHOLDING

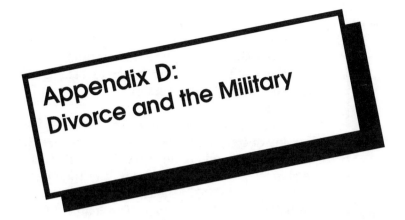

Appendix D:
Divorce and the Military

Divorce by or against a spouse in active-duty military service creates several special problems. Right away, there can be practical problems with locating and serving papers on the servicemember who may be stationed at a distant military base. The military has its own retirement plan and health care system which are unlike civilian ones and are often difficult to navigate. The military also has special benefits, like PX and commissary, that can be divided during divorce.

Military Relief Laws

By far the biggest problem posed by a divorce with a military spouse are the state and federal military relief laws protecting active-duty servicemembers. These relief laws protect both plaintiffs and defendants serving in the military. But they're a bigger problem for plaintiffs filing against defendant-servicemembers, as the following sections explain.

Federal Soldiers' and Sailors' Civil Relief Act of 1940 (SSCRA)

The federal SSCRA, which has the widest scope, covers servicemembers in the active duty of the U.S. military (see the sidebox for which personnel are covered by the SSCRA). The act offers several forms of relief to servicemembers protecting them from some kinds of debts, taxes, installment contracts, lawsuits, etc. The intent of the SSCRA is to protect servicemembers from these obligations so they can focus on their military duties.

More Information

The SSCRA covers all five service branches of the U. S. military:

- **Army**
- **Navy**
- **Marine Corps**
- **Air Force**
- **Coast Guard**

The act also covers officers of the Public Health Service assigned to duty with the Army and Navy.

The SSCRA protects servicemembers in the *active duty* of the U.S. military which are made up of two components:

Active component. Members of regular units (Regular Army, Regular Navy, etc.).

Reserve component. Servicemembers *activated* from the two segments of the military reserve:

- *Reserves.* Each service branch has its own reserve units (Army Reserve (Army), Naval Reserve (Navy), etc.).
- *National Guard.* State Army National Guard (attached to the Army) and Air National Guard (attached to the Air Force) units, including Michigan's army and air units.

Reservists are ordered to active duty selectively (call-up) for training, discipline or operations. Reservists can also be activated (mobilized), usually in unit strength, by the president in various ways (selective, partial, full or total mobilization) for a national emergency, such as war.

The SSCRA protects servicemembers lawfully away from active duty, such as during a period of leave or hospitalization.

The act covers military inductees (after receiving induction orders) and even pre-inductees who are receiving training or education preparing them for induction.

The SSCRA sometimes covers servicemembers' dependents, but not from lawsuits which is the focus here.

The act doesn't apply to civilians working for the military.

It's the lawsuit relief protections of the SSCRA that have an impact divorce. In essence, these protections shield servicemembers from hard-to-handle lawsuits, including divorces. There are two main lawsuit relief remedies:

Stay. During a lawsuit, a servicemember can ask for a stay or freezing of the case if s/he is serving outside the state where the lawsuit was filed. The court must grant the stay unless the member's ability to participate in the case isn't "materially affected" by military service. The length of the stay is up to the court, but it can last no more than 90 days beyond the end of military service. Typically, a stay will last only until the servicemember can get leave so s/he can deal with the lawsuit.

Reopening a default judgment. If a servicemember doesn't participate in the lawsuit, and a default judgment is ultimately issued, s/he can ask for reopening of the case. The request must be made no later than 90 days after the servicemember leaves military service. Reopening isn't guaranteed; the member must have a good defense and show that military service impaired his/her ability to take part in the case.

The SSCRA's lawsuit relief remedies are really designed for different situations. But sometimes a servicemember can use both remedies; other times using one means loss of the other. The SSCRA also allows a servicemember to waive (give up) these relief protections. The chart on the opposite page explains how these remedies fit together.

During peacetime, the SSCRA's lawsuit relief protections seldom totally bar a divorce against a servicemember. At a minimum, the act requires a little extra paperwork and the divorce can go through as smoothly as one against a civilian. At most, the divorce will be frozen until the servicemember can respond, either by obtaining leave or by separation from the service.

In a war, the SSCRA's stay remedy may be extended. For example, during the Persian Gulf War in 1990-91, SSCRA stays were expanded effectively freezing all lawsuits against active-duty servicemembers until after the war. This kind of total-but-temporary freeze could be used again in a future war or crisis.

SSCRA Lawsuit Relief Rights

	Right to request stay	Right to request reopening of default judgment
Defendant signs a waiver of SSCRA rights	No	No
Defendant asks court for a stay or other relief	Yes	No
Defendant doesn't respond:		
open case	Court may appoint a GAL,* who can ask for a stay or other relief	Yes
closed case	(2) Yes, if case is reopened	(1) Yes, then may ask for a stay

* GAL = *guardian ad litem*

Michigan Military Relief Law

Many people don't know it, but Michigan has a military relief law similar to the SSCRA. The state law covers Michigan National Guardmembers in active duty (see the sidebox for the extent of the law's coverage). Like the federal law, Michigan's law offers protection from some debt collection, foreclosures, utility shutoffs and lawsuits.

Unlike the SSCRA, Michigan's relief law offers absolute protection from lawsuits, without regard to hardship for the servicemember. After activation of guardmembers, Michigan's law effectively freezes lawsuits against them until termination of their active-duty service for the state.

More Information

Michigan's military relief law covers members in Michigan's two National Guard units:

• **Army National Guard**
• **Air National Guard**

The law protects guardmembers in *active duty* for more than seven days after activation by the governor: 1) to support civilian authority (such as during a riot, flood, etc.) 2) for a war or emergency of the state or nation.

The protections of the law extend beyond the period of active duty for some things, but not for lawsuit relief which is the focus here.

Note: Other states have similar military relief laws protecting their National Guardmembers which could be an issue if a party is in the active duty of an out-of-state unit.

Divorce by a Plaintiff-Servicemember

More Information

It can be difficult to find the address of active-duty servicemembers. But there are several resources that can help. For good general information, get:

How to Locate Anyone Who Is or Has Been in the Military: Armed Forces Locator Guide, 8th ed., Richard Johnson and Debra Knox, Spartanburg, SC: MIE Publishing, 1999, available from the publisher at (800) 937-2133 or through www.militaryusa.com.

If you know where the defendant is stationed, call the base locator (often just the information operator at the base). The Johnson and Knox book has a list of base locators telephone numbers for all military installations in the U.S. and worldwide. Besides finding the defendant, the base locator can also provide information about contacting the defendant's commanding officer for carrying out service.

When you know the defendant's service branch, contact the locator service for that branch. If you don't know which branch the defendant is serving in, contact all the military locators.

To make a location request, you need the defendant's full name and date of birth or social security number; other information like rank, service number and last duty assignment is helpful. The locators charge fees for requests, but these are sometimes waived for family member-requesters.

For convenience, a locator request form is included in this book: the Military Locator Request. This form addresses the five military locators and lists the fees they charge. If you're making multiple requests, photocopy extras as needed.

Send your locator requests to the military locators with the fees and a self-addressed stamped envelope. You will typically receive a response within a few weeks.

One problem with all the military locators is that they typically won't release current military addresses or duty assignments of troops overseas, aboard ships or in combat, for security reasons. You may be able to get around this problem if you know the overseas base or ship with the defendant. The Johnson and Knox book cited above has lists of all overseas military installations and Navy and Coast Guard ships and home ports. The book has suggestions about improvising addresses to servicemembers overseas or at sea using APO (American post office) and FPO (foreign post office) addresses.

You might get lucky and contact the defendant that way. If not, you will have to use a form of alternate service (see Appendix B for more about alternate service). Be sure to attach the (failed) locator response(s) to your motion for alternate service. The alternate service may involve service on the defendant's relatives who probably have his/her address.

Before filing, a plaintiff-servicemember must decide where to file. Choosing the correct state is known as jurisdiction (see "Can I Get a Divorce in Michigan?" on page 24 about jurisdiction), while choice of county inside Michigan is called venue (venue rules are covered in "Can I File the Divorce in My County?" on page 26). Both jurisdiction and venue are based on residence, or one's permanent home.

Special residence rules apply to military servicemembers. Ordinarily, servicemembers keep their pre-enlistment state and county residence. So if you were a Michigan resident before enlistment, you're still a resident of Michigan and your home county regardless of where you are stationed now. You may then file either in your old home county or the Michigan county where the defendant is residing now. If you have lost your Michigan residence, you must file in the Michigan county where the defendant lives.

Wherever you file, you can file by mail and have the divorce papers served by any of the service methods. Later on, other papers can be filed by mail and the divorce conducted long-distance.

The SSCRA protects whichever party—plaintiff or defendant—is in active-duty military service. A military plaintiff wouldn't invoke the act to block his/her own divorce, so the SSCRA seldom becomes an issue when the plaintiff is the servicemember.

There is one instance in which a plaintiff-servicemember might use the stay remedy of the act. At the end of the divorce, you must attend a final hearing in court and give brief testimony for the Judgment of Divorce. To make this appearance, you may need to obtain leave to return home. If leave can be arranged, the SSCRA will be satisfied and the divorce can be completed normally. But if you can't coordinate your leave with the court's hearing schedule, you could invoke the act's stay remedy and ask for rescheduling of the final hearing to coincide with your leave.

Divorcing a Defendant-Servicemember

Before you begin the divorce, choose the correct state (this choice is known as jurisdiction, and is covered in "Can I Get a Divorce in Michigan?" on page 24) and county (choice of county is known as venue; see "Can I File the Divorce in My County?" on page 26 for venue rules) for filing. Both jurisdiction and venue are based on residence, or one's permanent home.

There are special residence rules for servicemembers which can affect jurisdiction and venue. Ordinarily, servicemembers keep their pre-enlistment state and county residence, no matter how far away they are stationed now. So if the defendant resided in Michigan with you during your marriage just before entry into the service, there should be full Michigan jurisdiction.

For convenience, you will probably file in the Michigan county where you live now. But you may have another choice: defendant's pre-enlistment home county, since his/her residence continues there during the period of military service.

Before you can have the divorce papers served, you must know where the defendant is stationed. If you've lost touch, there are ways to find military personnel through a military locator service. The sidebox explains how to contact a base locator (when you know where the defendant is stationed) or a service branch locator (when you lack specific information).

The best way to serve a military spouse is by mail, since the U.S. Postal Service delivers mail (including certified mail necessary for service) to military bases all over the world. Military mail overseas can be a little slow, so allow extra time for service outside the country. See "Service" on page 67 for more about serving by mail and by the other service methods.

If a defendant is stationed at a stateside military base and refuses to accept mailed service, contact the sheriff or a commercial process server in the county and arrange for service by delivery. Military personnel living off base can be served at home without a problem. But except for the Air Force, most service branches don't allow process servers to enter military bases and serve servicemembers there directly. Instead, the defendant-servicemember's commanding officer sets up a time and place for service, if the member agrees to accept the papers; if s/he refuses service, the commanding officer notifies the server of the refusal. Sheriffs and commercial process servers in areas with military bases should be familiar with these service procedures.

Oddly, service can be easier at a military base in a foreign country. Overseas, commanding officers can carry out service, but are discouraged from acting as actual process servers. As a compromise, you can contact the

More Information

About military retirement benefits, health care coverage and other benefits (such as PX and commissary) available to a divorced non-military spouse, order for $10 the booklet "A Guide for Military Separation or Divorce" from:

Ex-Partners of Servicemembers for Equality (Ex-Pose)
P.O. Box 11191
Alexandria, VA 22312
(703) 941-5844

About division of military retirement pay from a servicemember's point of view, get:

Divorce and the Military II: A Comprehensive Guide for Service Members, Spouses, and Attorneys, 2nd ed., Marsha L. Thole and Frank W. Ault, Redlands, CA: The American Retirees Association, 2001

defendant's commander and suggest service by acknowledgment (see "Service by Acknowledgment" on page 68 for instructions). The commander can hand the service papers to the defendant, and ask for acknowledgment of service. If the defendant refuses service, the commanding officer cannot force service, and will notify you of the refusal.

Satisfying the Military Relief Laws

After service, you must come to grips with the military relief laws. If the defendant is protected by Michigan's military relief law, or if the SSCRA has put a temporary ban on all lawsuits, you can only proceed with a waiver from the defendant (see below on getting a waiver).

But typically, the defendant will be protected by the SSCRA's lawsuit relief remedies (stay and default judgment reopening). As explained before, these are flexible remedies which often allow divorces to go through. Here are several typical scenarios where the SSCRA is satisfied and the divorce can be completed.

Waiver of Military Relief Laws by the Defendant

As with other legal rights, a defendant-servicemember can voluntarily waive (give up) his/her lawsuit relief rights provided by the military relief laws. The waiver cuts off these rights, allowing the divorce to go through normally.

Waiver is the only way to satisfy Michigan's military relief law and the SSCRA when it has imposed a temporary wartime freeze on lawsuits. But even if the SSCRA applies in its normal peacetime form, waiver always makes it easier for the divorce to proceed.

If the defendant is willing to waive, send the Waiver of Military Relief Law Rights (GRP 6) to the defendant and have him/her sign the form. After you get the GRP 6 back, attach the form to the Default (GRP 2) as described in "Default and the Military Relief Laws" on page 79.

The Defendant Seeks a SSCRA Stay

After receiving the divorce papers, the defendant may contact the court and ask for a stay or other relief under the SSCRA. The defendant may ask for this personally, with the help of a legal assistance lawyer, which the military provides, or through a privately-retained lawyer. A stay request may be informal, such as a letter from the servicemember to the court, or a formal motion filed by the defendant's lawyer. In some cases, the court can even issue a stay on its own.

In considering a request for a stay, the judge must determine if the defendant's military service has a material effect on the servicemember's ability to participate in the case. Courts have defined material effect in terms of two main factors:

Financial hardship. Courts want to know if military service has caused a financial hardship for the servicemember, which has impaired the ability to respond. Military service often means a loss of income and extra financial obligations. On the other hand, some large employers make up the difference in pay and offer extra benefits to activated employees, resulting in no net loss of income. Under- or unemployed servicemembers may actually see an increase in income from military service.

Geographical distance. This is probably the most important factor. If the defendant-servicemember is at sea or stationed overseas, a good argument can be made that military service is hampering the defendant in the case. On the other hand, leave can cancel distance, since the servicemember can often use the leave to return home and participate in the case. Thus, the availability of leave is often the deciding issue for a stay request. It's also important for determining the length of the stay, if one is issued.

Sometimes, the defendant or his/her lawyer will include facts about financial hardship and distance (including availability of leave) in the stay request. Other times, the stay request may be brief, with few facts. If facts are sketchy, the court may not have enough information to rule on the request. You can step in and ask the defendant for the necessary information, including:

- When does your present enlistment expire?
- When do you expect to be released from active duty?
- When are you due to be transferred from you present duty station?
- Do you know where you will be assigned after you complete your current tour of duty?
- What ordinary or emergency leave do you have available?
- Describe any efforts you have made to obtain leave to participate in this case.
- If you joined active-duty service during the prior two years, what is the difference between your pre-service and in-service annual income?

You can ask for this information in an informal letter to the defendant or his/her lawyer. If the defendant won't respond, you can ask for this information from the defendant's commanding officers. It's customary to start with the defendant's immediate commander, and then work up the chain of command until you get a response. Any response received should be filed with the clerk, and brought to the attention of the judge if a stay becomes an issue.

If the court grants the defendant's stay request, the stay will merely delay the divorce, not end it. The court should grant the stay only until the defendant has time to deal with the divorce. This could be until the next period of leave, or when the defendant leaves the service, when separation is imminent. You can wait until the stay expires, and then resume the divorce where you left off.

If the stay is long, the clerk may try to dismiss the case for no progress. You can prevent dismissal by pointing out the stay to the clerk, and explain that this is the reason for delay in the case.

Whether a stay is granted or denied, the fact that the defendant (personally or through a lawyer) made the stay request is important. The stay request is regarded as the defendant's chief SSCRA remedy, and results in loss of the right to request reopening of any default judgment of divorce entered later.

As a result, when you the file the Default (GRP 2), check the second outdented box and the "other" box in paragraph #4, and then mention in the blank line that the defendant has requested a SSCRA stay. Bring this to the judge's attention also during your testimony at the final hearing.

The Defendant Doesn't Respond

It's more difficult dealing with an unresponsive defendant-servicemember. Your checking the second outdented box only in paragraph #4 of the Default (GRP 2) signals to the court that the defendant is in the military, but hasn't given up SSCRA protection by waiver or by requesting a stay. The court must then decide whether and how to protect the defendant under the act.

For an unresponsive defendant, the court can appoint a *guardian ad litem* (GAL), usually a local lawyer, to protect the defendant. Despite the appointment, a GAL doesn't directly represent the servicemember, who probably wasn't consulted about the appointment and may not know the GAL even exists (the member may not know about the GAL's appointment if s/he is cut off from normal communications, such as during combat or a tour of duty at sea).

Typically, a GAL will ask for a stay, but could seek other relief. A GAL's stay request is judged the same way as one from the defendant: A stay will be issued unless the defendant's military service doesn't materially affect his/her ability to participate in the case. If the court grants the GAL's stay request, you must wait for the stay to expire before resuming the case.

When a defendant-servicemember asks for a stay (personally or through a non-GAL lawyer), the member gives up the right to request for reopening a default judgment later. This rule doesn't apply to a GAL-requested stay, because of the peculiar relationship between the GAL and servicemember described above. An unresponsive defendant will also retain the right to ask for reopening if the court declined to appoint a GAL.

If an unstayed case goes forward to a default judgment, the defendant can request reopening the judgment. The defendant can make the request anytime while in military service and even within 90 days after leaving the service. Reopening of the case isn't automatic. The defendant must show both a good defense and some prejudice from military service to get back in the case.

If the case is reopened, the defendant may be able to participate right away. But if the defendant is still serving in the military, or just recently left the service, s/he can ask for a stay, to get extra time to defend. As with pre-judgment stays, the defendant must prove a material effect from military service on his/her ability to participate in the case to obtain a stay.

STATE OF MICHIGAN Circuit Court - Family Division COUNTY	WAIVER OF MILITARY RELIEF LAW RIGHTS	CASE NO.

Plaintiff (appearing *in propria persona*):		Defendant:
	v	

Defendant says:

1. I am in the active duty of the following unit of the U.S. military:
THE 333RD MILITARY POLICE COMPANY, MICHIGAN ARMY NATIONAL GUARD

2. I waive all lawsuit relief rights provided to me in this case by the Soldiers' and Sailors' Civil Relief Act of 1940 and/or Michigan's military relief law (MCL 32.517) or a similar military relief law from another state.

Date 4-1-89   Defendant *Dudley E. Lovelace*

GRP 6 (1/04)   WAIVER OF MILITARY RELIEF LAW RIGHTS

Military Locator Request

TO:

Army Worldwide Locator
U.S. Army Enlisted Records and Evaluation Center
8899 E. 56th St.
Indianapolis, IN 46249-5301
Fee: $3.50 payable by check or money to "Finance Officer"

HQ AFPC/MSIMD
550 C St. West, Suite 50
Randolph AFB, TX 78150-4752
Fee: $3.50 payable by check or money order to "DAO-DE RAFB"

World Wide Locator
Bureau of Naval Personnel
Pers-324D
2 Navy Annex
Washington, DC 20370-3240
Fee: $3.50 payable by check or money to "U.S. Treasurer"

Coast Guard Locator Service
Commanding Officer (RAS)
444 SE Quincy St.
Topeka, KS 66683-3591
Fee: $3.50 payable by check or money order to "U.S. Treasurer"

Headquarters U.S. Marine Corps
Personnel Management Support Branch (MMSB-17)
2008 Elliot Rd.
Quantico, VA 22134-5030
Fee: $3.50 payable by check or money to "U.S. Treasurer"

RE:

Case name __LOVELACE v. LOVELACE__

Case number __89-00501-DO__

Full name of defendant __DUDLEY ERNEST LOVELACE__

Defendant's date of birth __6-15-64__

Defendant's social security number __379-10-5567__

Defendant's rank and service number (if known) __—__

Defendant's last duty assignment (if known) __—__

Defendant's last military address (if known) __—__

I am the plaintiff in the above case seeking a divorce against the defendant. I request information about the defendant's current rank, service number, unit of assignment and military address. I need this information for service of process, to satisfy the military relief laws and other reasons related to this divorce case.

A self-addressed stamped envelope is enclosed for your response. A locator fee is also enclosed, but if I qualify for a fee waiver (as spouse), please refund my payment.

Date __3-15-89__

Signature __Darlene A. Lovelace__

Name __DARLENE A. LOVELACE__

Address __121 S. MAIN__

__LAKE CITY, MI 48800__

Telephone: __(517) 772-0000__

**Appendix E:
Dismissing Your Divorce**

If you and your spouse reconcile during the divorce, you may be anxious to dismiss the divorce immediately. But this may not always be wise. It takes a lot of work to file a divorce, so why jeopardize all your effort with a hasty dismissal? Wait a while and see if the reconciliation lasts. If it does, go ahead and dismiss your divorce as described below. But if your reconciliation fails, pick up the divorce where you left off and finish it.

At one time, it was possible to let a divorce remain in court for months or even years while the parties attempted reconciliation. These days, courts are under pressure to move cases along quickly, so they won't tolerate very much delay. Nevertheless, you probably could let your divorce sit for a few months. Just make sure that your proof of service is on file with the clerk or else the clerk may dismiss the case for no progress after the 91-day summons expiration period (see "Filing the Proof of Service" on page 75 for more about this danger).

After you decide that your reconciliation is going to last, go ahead and dismiss your divorce. To dismiss your uncontested divorce, fill out the Notice of Dismissal by Plaintiff section of the Dismissal (MC 09). Choose dismissal "without prejudice" because this makes it easier to file another divorce later should your marriage break down again. After you prepare the Dismissal (MC 09), file it with the clerk and send a copy to the defendant.

Incidentally, if your fees were suspended at the beginning of the divorce, you must deal with the fees again before you file the Dismissal (MC 09). At that time, the court can order a final fee exemption or require payment of the fees (see Appendix A for more about the fee exemption procedure).

Original - Court
1st copy - Applicant
Other copies - All appearing parties

CASE NO.

Approved, SCAO

STATE OF MICHIGAN
JUDICIAL DISTRICT
JUDICIAL CIRCUIT
COUNTY PROBATE

DISMISSAL

Court telephone no.

Court address

Plaintiff name(s) and address(es)

v

Defendant name(s) and address(es)

Defendant's attorney, bar no., address, and telephone no.

Plaintiff's attorney, bar no., address, and telephone no.

☒ **NOTICE OF DISMISSAL BY PLAINTIFF**   ☐ with   prejudice as to:
                                           ☒ without

1. Plaintiff/Attorney for plaintiff files this notice of dismissal of this case
   ☒ all defendants.
   ☐ the following defendant(s): _____

2. I certify, under penalty of contempt, that:
   a. This notice is the first dismissal filed by the plaintiff based upon or including the same claim against the defendant.
   b. All costs of filing and service have been paid.
   c. **No answer or motion has been served upon the plaintiff by the defendant** as of the date of this notice.
   d. A copy of this notice has been provided to the appearing defendant/attorney by ☒ mail ☐ personal service.

                                           Darlene A. Lovelace
                                           Plaintiff/Attorney signature

_7-1-89_
Date

☐ **STIPULATION TO DISMISS**   ☐ with   prejudice as to:
                                 ☐ without

I stipulate to the dismissal of this case
   ☐ all parties.
   ☐ the following parties: _____

                                           _____
                                           Plaintiff/Attorney signature
Date

                                           _____
                                           Defendant/Attorney signature
Date

☐ **ORDER TO DISMISS**   ☐ with   prejudice. Conditions, if any: _____
                           ☐ without

IT IS ORDERED this case is dismissed

_____

_____   Bar no.

                        Judge
Date   MCR 2.504

MC 09 (6/97) **DISMISSAL**

Appendix F:
Additional Judgment
Provisions

The first page of the Judgment of Divorce (GRP 4a) contains standard judgment provisions that should take care of most divorce cases without minor children. But in special cases, these standard provisions might not be enough.

Luckily, the judgment form is open-ended and expandable allowing you to add extra judgment provisions. If have you just a few additions, insert these in the blank space on the Judgment of Divorce (GRP 4e).* When you need more room, make photcopies of the GRP 4e and add these as extra pages. As you expand the judgment this way, remember to number the judgment pages consecutively in the captions of the forms.

If you're providing for alimony, use the Judgment of Divorce (GRP 4x). This form has a place for an alimony provision and the standard support provisions necessary for alimony. Sandwich the GRP 4x between the GRP 4a and GRP 4e, with the GRP 4x as the second page of the judgment and the GRP 4e as the third page.

The sections below deal with special situations in which you might need additional judgment provisions. Sample judgment provisions are also included which you can use or adapt to your case.

Property Division Provisions

Before you can provide for a property division in your judgment, you must do a complete inventory and valuation of your property (see "Can I Get a

---

* The omitted judgment pages (GRP 4b, c and d) have child custody, parenting time and child support provisions for cases with minor children, and therefore aren't included in this book.

Fair Property Division?" on page 31 for more about inventorying and valuing property). You and the defendant should also agree to an overall division of your property. If you have a prenuptial agreement dealing with divorce, this document will normally control the division. Otherwise, you must decide the shares each of you is to receive. Are you going to divide your property equally, 55-45, 60-40, etc.? After you do all those things, you're ready to begin the actual division of property.

Dividing Real Property

More Information

The court rules specify a judgment style which you must follow in adding provisions to your judgment:

- There must be only one subject or topic per judgment provision.

- All provisions must be numbered consecutively.

- All provisions must have a descriptive introductory heading, which is normally in bold on printed forms. However, you can underline introductory headings as a substitute for bold-face type.

All real property must be divided specifically in your divorce judgment. This rule applies both to real property owned by spouses jointly (joint real property) and real property that a spouse owns alone (solely-owned real property). The provisions below divide joint and solely-owned real property in three ways: 1) trade-off 2) buy-out (by one spouse from the other) 3) sale (to third parties). There are several other ways to divide real property, but these are far too complicated to do by yourself.

If you and your spouse don't own any real property, check the first box in paragraph #5A of the Judgment of Divorce (GRP 4a). If you are property-owners, check the second box and then divide the property in the Judgment of Divorce (GRP 4e).

As you divide real property, include the street address and legal description. Adding the legal description is important because this permits you to use the judgment as a substitute deed if one spouse refuses to sign a deed for the property (see "Transferring Property" on page 97 for more about using a judgment to transfer property this way). You can find the legal description in a deed, land contract, mortgage, abstract of title or title insurance policy for the property.

Joint Real Property

If you do nothing with joint real property in your divorce judgment, the property automatically converts to tenancy in common ownership. This might be acceptable for a while. As tenants in common, you and the defendant would each get an equal share of the property. If either of you were to die, your share would pass to your heirs/will beneficiaries, not your ex-spouse, because tenancy in common property doesn't have rights of survivorship.

But in the long run, tenancy in common ownership isn't practical for divorced persons. A tenancy in common is really like a partnership. Both tenants in common have an equal right to possess and use the property, and each has a duty to maintain it. This kind of close-knit arrangement is seldom suitable for ex-spouses.

Consequently, you should divide your joint real property in another way. The provisions below suggest several division options, some of which you may be able to handle yourself.

If enough property is available, one spouse can trade his/her share of the joint property for an equivalent amount of other property. For example, let's say that spouses jointly own a house worth $50,000 and have $50,000 of miscellaneous property. If the spouses agree to an equal property division, the defendant could trade his/her one-half share of the house for the plaintiff's half-interest in the miscellaneous property. After giving all the miscellaneous property to the defendant elsewhere in the property division, the spouses might use a provision like the one below to give the jointly-owned house to the plaintiff:

13. <u>Real Property</u>. Plaintiff is awarded the property located at 121 S. Main, Lake City, Michigan, and described below, free of any claims of defendant:

    Lot 2 of Assessor's Plat, Lake City, Ojibway County, Michigan

    Plaintiff shall be responsible for any indebtedness against the property and hold defendant harmless from liability for this debt.

Instead of a trade-off, one spouse could purchase the other's share of the joint real property. The provision below provides for a buy-out of the defendant's share by the plaintiff for cash:

13. <u>Real Property</u>. Plaintiff shall be awarded the property located at 121 S. Main, Lake City, Michigan, and described below, free of any claims of defendant, upon the payment of $25,000 to defendant:

    Lot 2 of Assessor's Plat, Lake City, Ojibway County, Michigan

    Plaintiff shall be responsible for any indebtedness against the property and hold defendant harmless from liability for this debt.

This provision lets the plaintiff buy out the defendant with a single cash payment. If the buyer-spouse can't afford to pay cash, s/he could make installment payments. But to provide for that type of buy-out, one must know about installment sales, how to secure them and their tax consequences. All these things are quite complicated, so seek legal help if you want to provide for a buy-out on an installment basis.

The sale of joint property to third parties is another way to handle joint property. You can arrange for an immediate sale at the time of your divorce or delay the sale until later. Either way, the sale provision will usually convert the joint property into a tenancy in common until the sale. Then, the provision will typically require: 1) pay-off of any mortgage or land contract against the property 2) payment of all selling costs (broker's commission, closing costs, etc.) 3) division of any remaining proceeds. A good sale provision should also say who shall possess and maintain the property before the sale. All these things are included in the immediate sale provision below:

13. <u>Real Property</u>. The property located at 121 S. Main, Lake City, Michigan, and described below, shall be owned by plaintiff and defendant as tenants in common:

Lot 2 of Assessor's Plat, Lake City, Ojibway County, Michigan

This property shall be sold as soon as possible at a price and terms the parties shall agree upon. After the property is sold, the proceeds of the sale shall be applied first to satisfy any indebtedness against the property, then against all the costs of sale (including any broker's commission and closing costs). Any remainder shall be divided [equally] between the parties.

Until the closing of the sale, plaintiff shall have sole possession of the property. Plaintiff shall be responsible for any mortgage or land contract payments, taxes, insurance and other expenses of maintaining the property during this time until the day of closing.

An immediate sale is simple and provides for a clean break between the spouses. There may also be sound tax reasons for selling real property around the time of a divorce, especially when the property is the former marital home. However, an immediate sale may displace a parent and children living at the home.

A delayed sale can solve that problem. It can permit the in-home parent to live in the former marital home for a while, yet will eventually allow the other parent to receive his/her share of the property when the delayed sale occurs. The trouble is, a delayed sale is difficult to provide for in a judgment. The events triggering the delayed sale (remarriage of the in-home parent, maturity of children, etc.) must be anticipated and carefully described in the provision. The other parent may want interest on his/her share of the property, and have it protected by a mortgage or other security. Finally, the income tax consequences from a delayed sale can be unfavorable. For all these reasons, if you want a delayed sale, go to a lawyer for help.

Solely-Owned Real Property

If you fail to deal with solely-owned real property in your judgment, the owner-spouse retains ownership of the property free of any claim or interest of the other spouse (in part, that's what paragraph #6 of the Judgment of Divorce (GRP 4a) is about). But you shouldn't leave it at that. Even if you want the owner-spouse to keep his/her solely-owned property (presumably because of a trade-off or buy-out), you should say so in your judgment. When you want another disposition of the property, such as a sale to a third party, you must provide for that as well.

In this case, the nonowner is trading off his/her hypothetical share in the owner-spouse's solely-owned real property for equivalent property elsewhere in the property division. The owner-spouse keeps ownership of the property:In this case, the nonown

13. <u>Real Property</u>. Plaintiff is awarded the property located at 121 S. Main, Lake City, Michigan, and described below, free of any claims of defendant:

Lot 2 of Assessor's Plat, Lake City, Ojibway County, Michigan

Plaintiff shall be responsible for any indebtedness against the property and hold defendant harmless from liability for this debt.

The owner-spouse buys out the nonowner's "share" in his/her solely-owned real property for cash:*

13. <u>Real Property</u>. Plaintiff shall be awarded the property located at 121 S. Main, Lake City, Michigan, and described below, free of any claims of defendant, upon the payment of $25,000 to defendant:

Lot 2 of Assessor's Plat, Lake City, Ojibway County, Michigan

Plaintiff shall be responsible for any indebtedness against the property and hold defendant harmless from liability for this debt.

In this scenario, the solely-owned property must be sold as soon as possible to a third party followed by a division of the proceeds:**

13. <u>Real Property</u>. The property located at 121 S. Main, Lake City, Michigan, and described below, shall be owned by plaintiff and defendant as tenants in common:

Lot 2 of Assessor's Plat, Lake City, Ojibway County, Michigan

This property shall be sold as soon as possible at a price and terms the parties shall agree upon. After the property is sold, the proceeds of the sale shall be applied first to satisfy any indebtedness against

---

*   As an alternative, you can provide for an installment sale. But as explained above, that's probably too difficult for you to arrange yourself.

**   Instead of an immediate sale, you could choose a delayed sale. Yet, as mentioned above, you will probably need legal help to provide for that arrangement.

the property, then against all the costs of sale (including any broker's commission and closing costs). Any remainder shall be divided [equally] between the parties.

Until the closing of the sale, plaintiff shall have sole possession of the property. Plaintiff shall be responsible for any mortgage or land contract payments, taxes, insurance and other expenses of maintaining the property during that time until the day of closing.

Dividing Personal Property

You may have already divided the bulk of your personal property, such as clothing, household goods, bank accounts and motor vehicles, during or even before your divorce. Courts usually permit informal divisions of personal property because they know that you cannot wait until the end of your divorce to divide essential items. If you have already divided some or all of your personal property that way, confirm the division by checking the first box in paragraph #5B of the Judgment of Divorce (GRP 4a).

On the other hand, you should specifically mention personal property that hasn't yet been transferred to the intended recipient at the time of your final hearing. This avoids confusion about ownership later. For example, if you and the defendant have agreed that the defendant must give you an automobile, a dinette set and a $1,000 bank account, you should say so in your judgment. Check the second box in paragraph #5B of the Judgment of Divorce (GRP 4a), and include this provision in the Judgment of Divorce (GRP 4e):

13. <u>Personal Property</u>. Plaintiff is awarded the following personal property free of any claims of defendant:

     1984 Dodge Aries automobile VIN VL29C4B266259

     Five-piece (table and four chairs) Contemporary dinette set

     Ojibway State Bank savings account #00012400-001, with a current balance of $1,000

     Plaintiff shall be responsible for any indebtedness against this property and hold defendant harmless from liability for this debt.

You can adapt this provision to divide almost any type of personal property. But use it only for the distribution of important items of personal property. Don't clutter up your judgment by mentioning every piece of furniture or article of clothing.

Whenever you use such a provision, include a complete description of the property since this aids transfer of the item later (see "After Your Divorce" on page 97 for more information about transferring property). Describe the property fully and mention any identification numbers (account numbers for financial accounts, vehicle identification numbers (VINs) for automobiles, hull numbers for boats, etc.), as in the example above.

Dividing Retirement Benefits, Businesses and Other New Property

A divorce property division isn't complete without considering so-called new property (retirement benefits, businesses, etc.). The problem is, new property is often difficult to divide. Unlike a house or an automobile, you can't put retirement benefits on the market, sell them and divide the proceeds (most retirement plans prohibit this kind of sale or transfer even if you could find a buyer).

A business can also be hard to liquidate. Some one-person businesses depend on the skill of their owner-operators and may be impossible to sell as going concerns. And even when a small business can be sold, it must often be sold as a piece because few people will buy a share of a small business.

Despite these problems, the law has devised ways to divide new property, often without actually distributing it.

Dividing Retirement Benefits

Michigan courts have approved two methods for dividing retirement benefits: 1) trade-off 2) division of payments.

In a trade-off, the nonemployee-spouse trades his/her interest in the retirement benefits for a like share of other property. As an example, let's assume that a couple owns an automobile worth $10,000 and the husband has retirement benefits with a present value of $10,000. If the spouses agree to an equal property division, the wife might trade her one-half interest in the retirement benefits for the husband's half-interest in the automobile. Thus, the retirement benefits stay with the husband, but the wife gets the automobile. By this means, the retirement benefits have been divided, but without actually distributing them.

The other method of division—division of payments—results in the actual distribution of the retirement benefits to both spouses. With this method, the retirement benefits are divided fractionally between the spouses as payments are made. For example, if the husband is receiving monthly payments, and the parties want an equal division of property, they could assign one-half of the payments to each spouse monthly.

Each of these methods has pluses and minuses. Trade-off is nice because it gives the nonemployee-spouse value immediately, without waiting for the retirement plan to mature (pay benefits). But it requires an estimation of the present value of the benefits, which is complicated (see "Can I Get a Fair Property Division?" on page 31 for more about the valuation of retirement plans). Trade-off also places the risk that the employee-spouse will never collect the benefits (because of premature death, early retirement, discharge, bankruptcy of the employer, etc.) on the employee-spouse alone. If the employee-spouse never gets benefits, s/he has traded off other property for nothing. Finally, a trade-off may be impossible if the value of the retirement benefits is great and there is no other property that can be traded for them.

It's simpler to just divide the retirement benefits. Unlike a trade-off, you normally won't have to estimate the total value of the benefits, since your dividing the payments, not the total benefits package. This avoids making a difficult present value calculation. Dividing payments also spreads the risks associated with the retirement benefits to both spouses. If the retirement plan fails, both spouses share the loss; if benefits increase in the future, each spouse shares in the gain.

But unless the retirement plan is mature (paying benefits), dividing payments often won't give the nonemployee-spouse any property immediately after the divorce. What's more, a division-of-payments order is difficult to provide for in a divorce judgment. You must use precise language or it won't be legally effective. For this reason, if you want to divide retirement benefits during divorce yourself, you will have to use the trade-off method. To do that, simply check the first box in paragraph #8 of your Judgment of Divorce (GRP 4a), and then give or get equivalent property elsewhere in the property division. If you want to use the division-of-payments method, see a lawyer.

Individual retirement arrangements (IRAs), which are individual retirement plans, can be divided in several ways, including: 1) transfer from the owner-spouse to the other spouse 2) trade-off 3) withdrawal and division of the proceeds.

To transfer an IRA, describe the account and provide for transfer in a judgment provision, like the bank account example on page 158. This kind of divorce-related transfer isn't considered a withdrawal, so no tax or early withdrawal penalty is imposed. But tax and an early withdrawal penalty may be due if the new owner of the account withdraws money from it prematurely. If you want to trade off an IRA for other property, make sure that you have checked the first box in paragraph #8 of your Judgment of Divorce (GRP 4a), and give the nonowner-spouse equivalent property elsewhere in the judgment. You can also withdraw the money in an IRA and divide it. But if the IRA-owner is younger than 59½, that's a premature withdrawal and a penalty will be imposed.

Keogh (HR-10) plans are another type of individual retirement plan. Like IRAs, these plans can be transferred, traded or withdrawn and divided. But transferring or withdrawing Keoghs can have bad tax consequences, leaving trade-off as the best method of division in most cases.

Dividing Businesses and Other New Property

Business interests can be transferred between spouses or liquidated and divided. In many cases, trade-off is the best method of division. To trade off a business, create a judgment provision like the one below, assigning the business to the business-owner, and then give the nonbusiness-owner equivalent property elsewhere in the property division.

13. <u>Personal Property</u>. Defendant is awarded all the assets, including inventory, supplies, fixtures, equipment, accounts and goodwill, in the House of Waterbeds, Lake City, Michigan, free of any claims of plaintiff. Defendant shall hold plaintiff harmless from any liability in connection with this business.

Division of Debts

As you end your marriage, who is responsible for debts you leave behind? If you do nothing, the following general rules govern liability for sole debts (debts incurred by a spouse alone) and joint debts (debts taken on by spouses together):

Sole debt. The spouse who incurred the debt (debtor-spouse) remains liable for it after the divorce. The nondebtor-spouse generally won't be liable for the debt unless s/he gave the debtor-spouse authority, as an agent, to incur debts of the nondebtor-spouse's behalf. The agent's authority can be express, implied or even given after the fact, by ratification of what the debtor-spouse did.

Joint debt. Because both spouses incurred joint debts, each remains liable for these after divorce.

By dividing debts in your divorce judgment, you can modify this liability to an extent. A debt provision can shift the liability for a sole debt from the debtor-spouse to the other spouse. It could also have one spouse assume liability for a joint debt or a sole debt for which both spouses are liable under the agent exception described above.

Not all debts may be reassigned that way. Educational and personal loans are better left with those incurring them, since they have a bigger incentive to pay them. Likewise, debts secured by property (mortgages, land contracts and other liens) are customarily transferred to the recipients of the secured property. (For this reason, all the sample property division provisions in this appendix transfer secured debts together with the property securing them.) On the other hand, general unsecured debts, such as credit card or charge account debts, are good choices for division.

Whatever you decide, any debt provision you insert in your judgment must describe the debt and say who is responsible for paying it, as in the following provision:

13. <u>Debts</u>. Defendant is responsible for, and must hold plaintiff harmless from, the following debts:

Lake City Department Store charge account #22224445 with a current balance of $540

Mastercredit account #5215 0200 3400 6529 with a current balance of $1,233.33

Debt Division and Creditors' Rights

Although you and the defendant can rearrange debts in your judgment, your arrangements won't affect the rights of the creditors holding the debts. Your creditors will have the same rights after your divorce as they had before.*

Example: A couple got a joint car loan from a bank (creditor). In their divorce, the wife received ownership of the car and the car loan was assigned to her by a debt provision in the divorce judgment. She falls behind on the car payments. The bank could sue the husband because the debt division didn't affect his liability to the bank.

Glossary

Indemnity–legal claim making someone else answerable for your obligation to a third person.

If a debt division doesn't change creditors' rights, why go to the trouble of dividing debts in your divorce judgment? The advantage to debt division is that it provides a legal claim, known as indemnity, against the spouse assuming the debt. The indemnity can then be used as a defense or as a direct claim.

Example: A couple gets a joint car loan from a bank (creditor). In their divorce, the wife gets the car and agrees to pay the loan off in a debt division provision. After she falls behind in car payments, the bank sues both spouses. The husband could cite the indemnity from the debt division and shift liability to the wife. Had the bank sued the husband alone, he could add the wife to the case and raise the indemnity against her this way.

Alimony Provisions

Every divorce judgment must deal with alimony** and settle the issue for *both* spouses by either: 1) waiving (giving up) 2) reserving 3) or granting alimony.

When you want to waive alimony for you or the defendant, indicate in paragraph #4 of your Judgment of Divorce (GRP 4a) that alimony is "not granted for" that particular party. By making that choice, you permanently

---

*   A creditor can agree to release a spouse from liability for a joint debt. In that case, the released spouse would no longer be liable to the creditor for the debt. Nevertheless, most creditors won't consent to such releases because they prefer to have two debtors rather than one.

**   In the judgment, alimony is called by its real name: spousal support.

waive alimony for the party whose box you have checked, and s/he won't be permitted to seek alimony later.

If you want to leave the issue of alimony open for a party, check the box indicating that alimony is "reserved for" that party. You cannot reserve alimony merely because you find the issue of alimony bothersome and don't want to deal with it now. To reserve alimony, you must have a good reason for the reservation, such as: 1) there is only limited jurisdiction in the case (see "Can I Get a Divorce in Michigan?" on page 24 about why limited jurisdiction isn't enough for alimony) 2) the payer is elusive or has disappeared and you cannot determine his/her ability to pay alimony 3) the would-be recipient of the alimony is making a personal or career change and isn't sure of his/her financial needs now. When alimony is reserved for a party, s/he can come back to court later and ask for alimony. At that time, the court will decide whether it should be paid.

If you and the defendant have agreed on some type of alimony, check the box in paragraph #4 of the GRP 4a that says alimony is "granted elsewhere in this judgment for" the recipient. You must then include an alimony provision somewhere else in the judgment. You can add the alimony provision in a special judgment expansion page, the Judgment of Divorce (GRP 4x).

When you're dealing with alimony in your judgment, make sure that you settle it for both parties in one of the three ways described above. If you fail to settle alimony for a party, the failure automatically reserves alimony for that party, allowing him/her to ask for it later.

The alimony provisions below are for short- and long-term alimony. Both provisions make the alimony subject to several conditions. You can omit any of these or add others. But keep in mind that the death-of-the-recipient condition is necessary to qualify the payments as alimony for federal tax purposes. Without that condition, the payments won't be deductible by the payer.

Short-Term Alimony

13. <u>Spousal Support</u>.   Defendant shall pay to plaintiff $200 monthly in advance on the first day of the month. This spousal support shall be modifiable. Payment of the support shall begin on September 7, 1989, and end immediately on the happening of any of the following events:

    (a) [September 7, 1991]

    (b) death of plaintiff

    (c) death of defendant

    (d) remarriage of plaintiff

    (e) cohabitation by plaintiff with a member of the opposite sex

    After plaintiff's spousal support ends, it shall be forever barred to her.

Long-Term Alimony

13. <u>Spousal Support</u>. Defendant shall pay to plaintiff $200 monthly in advance on the first day of the month. This spousal support shall be modifiable. Payment of the support shall begin on September 7, 1989, and end immediately on the happening of any of the following events:

(a) death of plaintiff

(b) death of defendant

(c) remarriage of plaintiff

(d) cohabitation by plaintiff with a member of the opposite sex

After plaintiff's spousal support ends, it shall be forever barred to her.

Alimony-Related Support Provisions

When you provide for alimony, you must add several provisions to your judgment. These are standard provisions required whenever support, such as alimony, is ordered. They include a general ban on retroactive modification of support, enforcement of past-due support by lien and surcharge, friend of the court service fees, if any, and a personal information section.

These extra support provisions have been gathered into an expansion page, the Judgment of Divorce (GRP 4x). You can add this page as the second page of your judgment. If there's enough room, you can put the alimony provision in paragraph #13 of the GRP 4x and select the method of payment in paragraph #14.

Choosing an Alimony Payment Method

Besides the alimony provision, and the standard support provisions cited above, you must set up a method of paying the alimony. As with the other kind of support, child support, the normal way of paying alimony is by immediate income withholding to the SDU. With this method, the alimony payer's source of income (usually an employer) deducts alimony from the payer's wages or salary and sends the money to the state disbursement unit (SDU) in Lansing, which forwards it to the alimony recipient. The friend of the court monitors payment, so it can enforce the obligation.

To obtain immediate income withholding, you must use an Income Withholding Order (FOC 5), and choose payment by immediate income withholding, payable to the SDU, in paragraph #14 of the Judgment of Divorce (GRP 4x). In Wayne County only, you must use an extra support form: Order Data Form-Support, which you can get at the Wayne County Clerk's office (the form comes with instructions).

Other Methods of Payment

Immediate income withholding is popular with alimony recipients and the courts because it makes alimony easy to collect. On the other hand, some alimony payers dislike it because it creates more paperwork for their employers. They may want to avoid immediate income withholding and set up a different method of payment.

If alimony isn't immediately withheld, the payer can pay it to the SDU or directly to the alimony recipient. Alimony payers may like payment to the recipient because it's informal with less paperwork. But recipients usually prefer payment to the SDU, since this offers better collection, record-keeping and enforcement of the alimony.

You can choose these other options by opting out of the friend of the court system. You can do a limited opt-out from immediate income withholding and choose another payment method, or elect another payment method as part of a broader (total or partial) opt-out from the friend of the court system. Appendix C has complete information about other payment options.

STATE OF MICHIGAN Circuit Court - Family Division COUNTY	JUDGMENT OF DIVORCE Page 2 of **3** pages	CASE NO.

Plaintiff: v   Defendant:

IT IS ALSO ORDERED:

13. **SPOUSAL SUPPORT:** DEFENDANT SHALL PAY TO PLAINTIFF $200 MONTHLY IN ADVANCE ON THE FIRST DAY OF THE MONTH. THIS SPOUSAL SUPPORT SHALL BE MODIFIABLE. PAYMENT OF THE SUPPORT SHALL BEGIN ON SEPT. 7, 1989, AND END IMMEDIATELY ON THE HAPPENING OF ANY OF THE FOLLOWING EVENTS:

(a) SEPT. 7, 1991

(b) DEATH OF PLAINTIFF

(c) DEATH OF DEFENDANT

(d) REMARRIAGE OF PLAINTIFF

(e) COHABITATION BY PLAINTIFF WITH A MEMBER OF THE OPPOSITE SEX

AFTER PLAINTIFF'S SPOUSAL SUPPORT ENDS, IT SHALL BE FOREVER BARRED TO HER.

14. **PAYMENT OF SUPPORT:** Spousal support shall be paid
by ☒ immediate income withholding   ☐ without income withholding until past-d[ue] equals or exceeds the monthly amount o[f]
to ☒ state disbursement unit (SDU).   ☐ directly to the payee.   ☐ other:

> THIS IS SHORT-TERM ALIMONY; SEE "ALIMONY PROVISIONS" IN APPENDIX F FOR LONG-TERM ALIMONY

15. **PAST-DUE SUPPORT:**

a. **Retroactive modification.** Support is an order the date it is due and shall not be modified retroac[tive]ly except as allowed by MCL 552.603 and 552.603b.

b. **Lien and surcharge.** Unpaid support is a lien on the payer's property by operation of law and the payer's property can be encumbered or seized if past-due support exceeds two times the monthly amount of periodic support payments. In a friend of the court case, a surcharge will be added to past-due support as provided by MCL 552.603a.

16. **FRIEND OF THE COURT SERVICES AND FEES:**

☐ a. **Friend of the court opt-out.** This case shall be opted out of the following friend of the court services: ☐ all friend of the court services   ☐ all friend of the court services except collection and distribution of spousal support through the SDU   ☐ immediate income withholding only

b. **Friend of the court fees.** While a friend of the court case, the support payer shall pay friend of the court service fees and other statutory fees.

17. **PERSONAL INFORMATION:** The parties' current residence addresses and telephone nos. appear in the main caption of this judgment. Their current sources of income are listed below:

	Plaintiff	Defendant
Source of income:	10,000 PANCAKES	WATERBED WORLD
Address:	III M-78 LAKE CITY, MI 48800	1000 SERVICE RD. LAKE CITY, MI 48800
Telephone no:	772-0011	773-0011

The parties have previously provided information about their health care coverage, social security nos., driver's and occupational licenses. In a friend of the court case, they must inform the friend of the court of any changes or additions to the personal information cited in this section, reporting changes in their residence information in writing within 21 days of a change.

GRP 4x (1/04)   JUDGMENT OF DIVORCE, page 2

Approved, SCAO

| STATE OF MICHIGAN
JUDICIAL CIRCUIT
COUNTY | Original - Court
1st copy - Friend of the Court

INCOME WITHHOLDING ORDER
☒ Court ordered   ☐ Consent | 2nd copy - Plaintiff
3rd copy - Defendant
Additional copies to all sources of income

CASE NO. |

Friend of the Court address

Plaintiff's name and address

Court telephone no.

v

Defendant's name and address

Regarding: **DUDLEY E. LOVELACE**
Payer

379-10-5567
Social security number

Date of order: **5-7-89**

Judge: **LESTER TUBBS**

1. The court finds that the above payer owes current support, statutory fees, and/or arrearages in the above case, and notice has been given as required by law.

2. Income is defined as: commissions, earnings, salaries, wages, and other income due now or in the future from an employer and successor employers; any payment due now or in the future from a profit-sharing plan, pension plan, insurance contract, annuity, unemployment compensation, supplemental unemployment benefits, and worker's compensation; any amount of money due the payer under a support order as a debt of any other individual, partnership, association, private or public corporation, the United States or any Federal agency, any state or political subdivision of any state, or any other legal entity indebted to the payer.

IT IS ORDERED:

3. The source of income shall withhold payer's income as specified in the attached notice of income withholding and in any subsequent notices.

4. The State Disbursement Unit shall receive and disburse these funds for the purpose of collecting support, statutory fees, and the payment of all arrearages.

5. Any income withheld under this order shall be paid to the State Disbursement Unit within 3 days after the date of withholding.

6. If the payer's existing support order is modified by an order of the court, the office of the friend of the court shall send a notice of modification to the source of income by ordinary mail. The amount assigned or withheld shall be changed to conform with the court modification within 7 days after receipt of the notice of modification.

Signature of preparer *Darlene A. Lovelace*

☐ I consent to the terms of this order.

Payer's signature

Judge *Lester Tubbs*

Bar no.

CERTIFICATE OF MAILING

I certify that on this date I mailed a copy of this order to the parties and sources of income by ordinary mail addressed to their last known addresses.

Date

Signature

FOC 5 (4/01) **INCOME WITHHOLDING ORDER**

MCL 552.601 et seq.; MSA 25.164(1) et seq

Regular Forms

Summons and Complaint	MC 01
Complaint for Divorce	GRP 1
Default	GRP 2
Notice of Entry of Default and Request for Default Judgment of Divorce	GRP 3
Judgment of Divorce	GRP 4a&e
Testimony	
Proof of Mailing	MC 302

Note: To remove the forms cleanly from the book, follow these steps: 1) keep the back of the book as flat as possible on a table or other hard surface 2) open the front of the book at the form you want to remove and tug gently on the form, keeping the back of the book flat.

Optional and Local Forms

Approved, SCAO

REQUEST FOR ACCOMMODATIONS	Court name and location

Today's date	**Instructions for completing form:** *Provide your name, address, and telephone number. Check the boxes which apply to you and provide any necessary details. When you have completed this request, please return it to the court at the above address.*

1.
Name

Address

City	State	Zip	Telephone no.

2. Court activity you need accommodations for:

☐ Hearing _____
Date

☐ Mediation meeting _____
Date

☐ Jury duty _____
Date(s)

☐ Other (specify): _____
include dates if relevant

3. What is the nature of your disability?

☐ Physical mobility impairment (wheelchair, walker, crutches, etc.)

☐ Speech impairment (specify): _____

☐ Visual impairment

☐ Hearing impairment (specify)   ☐ deaf   ☐ hard of hearing

☐ Other (specify): _____

4. What type of accommodation are you requesting?

☐ Interpreter for deaf (specify whether ASL, tactile, oral, etc.) _____

☐ Assistive listening device (specify type of device) _____

☐ Physical location accessible for persons with a physical mobility concern.

☐ Other (specify) _____

For court use only

MC 70 (10/97) **REQUEST FOR ACCOMMODATIONS**

Original - Court file
1st copy - Assignment Clerk/Extra
2nd copy - Friend of the Court/Extra
3rd copy - Opposing party
4th copy - Moving party

Approved, SCAO

STATE OF MICHIGAN JUDICIAL DISTRICT JUDICIAL CIRCUIT COUNTY	MOTION AND ORDER FOR APPOINTMENT OF FOREIGN LANGUAGE INTERPRETER	CASE NO.

Court address   Court telephone no.

Plaintiff name(s) ☐ moving party		Defendant name(s) ☐ moving party
Plaintiff's attorney, bar no., address, and telephone no.	v	Defendant's attorney, bar no., address, and telephone no.

MOTION

1. I state that I am unable to speak English sufficiently to understand and participate in the proceedings in this case.

2. ☐ I am represented by an attorney.   ☐ I am not represented by an attorney.

3. I request the court to appoint a foreign language interpreter to interpret for me.

4. I request an interpreter who speaks the _____ language.

5. If required, place my request on the motion calendar.

_____
Date

_____
Signature

To be completed only if the court
requires a hearing on the motion

NOTICE OF HEARING

You are notified that a hearing has been scheduled on this matter for:

Judge	Bar no.	Date	Time
Hearing location			
☐ Court address above ☐			

If you require special accommodations to use the court because of disabilities, please contact the court immediately to make arrangements.

_____
Date

_____
Signature

CERTIFICATE OF MAILING

I certify that on this date I mailed a copy of this motion and notice of hearing (if applicable) to the other party at the last known address.

_____
Date

_____
Signature

ORDER

IT IS ORDERED the above motion is   ☐ granted.   ☐ denied.

_____
Date

_____
Judge

MC 81 (10/01)   **MOTION AND ORDER FOR APPOINTMENT OF FOREIGN LANGUAGE INTERPRETER**

STATE OF MICHIGAN JUDICIAL DISTRICT JUDICIAL CIRCUIT COUNTY PROBATE	AFFIDAVIT AND ORDER SUSPENSION OF FEES/COSTS	CASE NO.

Court address

Court telephone no.

Plaintiff/Petitioner name, address, and telephone no.		Defendant/Respondent name, address, and telephone no.
	v	
Plaintiff's/Petitioner's attorney, bar no., address, and telephone no.		Defendant's/Respondent's attorney, bar no., address, and telephone no.

☐ Probate   In the matter of _____

NOTE: Requests for waiver/suspension of transcript costs must be made separately by motion.

AFFIDAVIT

1. The attached pleading is to be filed with the court by or on behalf of _____ ,
Name

applicant, who is ☐ plaintiff/petitioner.   ☐ defendant/respondent.

2. The applicant is entitled to and asks the court for suspension of fees and costs in the action for the following reason:

☐ a. S/he is currently receiving public assistance: $ _____ per _____ Case No.: _____ .

☐ b. S/he is unable to pay those fees and costs because of indigency, based on the following facts:

INCOME: _____
Employer name and address

_____ _____ _____ per ☐ week. ☐ month. ☐ two weeks.
Length of employment   Average gross pay   Average net pay

ASSETS: State value of car, home, bank deposits, bonds, stocks, etc.

OBLIGATIONS: Itemize monthly rent, installment payments, mortgage payments, child support, etc.

☐ 3. (in domestic relations cases only) The applicant is entitled to an order requiring his/her spouse to pay attorney fees.

REIMBURSEMENT: It is understood that the court may order the applicant to pay the fees and costs when the reason for their waiver or suspension no longer exists.

_____
Affiant signature

Subscribed and sworn to before me on _____ , _____ County, Michigan.
Date

My commission expires: _____ Signature: _____
Date   Deputy clerk/Register/Notary public

(SEE REVERSE SIDE FOR ORDER)

CERTIFICATION OF ATTORNEY

1. I have reviewed the affidavit of indigency, and I certify that its contents are true to the best of my information, knowledge, and belief.

2. I will bring to the court's attention the matter of suspended costs and fees and the availability of funds to pay them before any disposition is entered. I will report at that time any changes in the information contained in the affidavit of indigency or any other information regarding the affiant's financial status or alterations of the fee arrangement.

_____
Date

_____
Attorney signature

_____
Attorney name (type or   Bar no.
print)

CERTIFICATION BY PERSON OTHER THAN PARTY

1. I have personal knowledge of the facts appearing in the affidavit.

2. The person in whose behalf the petition is filed is unable to sign it because of

☐ minority: _____   ☐ other disability: _____
            Date of birth   Nature of disability

Relationship: _____

_____
Date

_____
Affiant signature

_____
Affiant name (type or print)

_____
Address

_____
City, state, zip   Telephone no.

ORDER

IT IS ORDERED:

☐ 1. Fees and costs in this action required by law or court rule are waived/suspended until further order of the court. Before any final disposition or discontinuance is entered, the moving party shall bring the fee and costs suspension to the attention of the judge for final disposition.

☐ 2. The applicant's spouse shall pay the fees and costs required by law or court rule.

☐ 3. This application is denied.

_____
Date

_____
Judge   Bar no.

STATE OF MICHIGAN JUDICIAL DISTRICT JUDICIAL CIRCUIT	MOTION AND VERIFICATION FOR ALTERNATE SERVICE	CASE NO.

Court address   Court telephone no.

Plaintiff name(s), address(es), and telephone number(s)		Defendant name(s), address(es), and telephone number(s)
	v	

1. Service of process upon _____ cannot reasonably be made as otherwise provided in MCR 2.105, as shown in the following verification of process server.

2. Defendant's last known home and business addresses are:

_____
Home address   City   State   Zip

_____
Business address   City   State   Zip

    a. I believe the ☐ home / ☐ business address shown above is current.

    b. I do not know defendant's current ☐ home / ☐ business address. I have made the following efforts to ascertain the

    current address: _____

    _____

    _____

3. I request the court order service by alternate means.

I declare that the statements above are true to the best of my information, knowledge and belief.

_____   _____
Date   Attorney signature

_____   _____
Address   Attorney name (type or print)   Bar no.

_____   _____
City, state, zip   Telephone no.

VERIFICATION OF PROCESS SERVER

1. I have tried to serve process on this defendant as described: State date, place, and what occurred on each occasion

I declare that the statements above are true to the best of my information, knowledge and belief.

_____   _____
Date   Signature

                                                 _____
                                               Process Server (type or print)

MC 303 (6/86)   **MOTION AND VERIFICATION FOR ALTERNATE SERVICE**   MCR 2.105

Approved, SCAO

STATE OF MICHIGAN JUDICIAL DISTRICT JUDICIAL CIRCUIT	ORDER FOR ALTERNATE SERVICE	CASE NO.

Court address _____   Court telephone no.

Plaintiff name(s), address(es), and telephone no.(s)	v	Defendant name(s), address(es), and telephone no.(s)

Plaintiff's attorney, bar no., address, and telephone no.

THE COURT FINDS:

1. Service of process upon defendant _____

   cannot reasonably be made as provided in MCR 2.105, and service of process may be made in a manner which is reasonably

   calculated to give defendant actual notice of the proceedings and an opportunity to be heard.

IT IS ORDERED:

2. Service of the summons and complaint and a copy of this order may be made by the following method(s):

   a. ☐ First class mail to _____

   b. ☐ Tacking or firmly affixing to the door at _____

   c. ☐ Delivering at _____

      to a member of defendant's household who is of suitable age and discretion to receive process, with instructions to deliver

      it promptly to defendant.

   d. ☐ Other: _____

      _____

3. For each method used, proof of service must be filed promptly with the court.

_____   _____
Date   Judge   Bar no.

MC 304 (3/00) **ORDER FOR ALTERNATE SERVICE**   MCR 2.103, MCR 2.105

PROOF OF SERVICE

I served a copy of the summons and complaint and a copy of the order for alternate service upon

by: _____

1. First class mail to _____, on _____
                                                                   Date

2. Tacking or firmly affixing to the door at _____, on _____
                                                                   Date

3. Delivering at _____, on _____
                                                                   Date

to a member of defendant's household who is of suitable age and discretion to receive process, with instructions to deliver it promptly to defendant.

4. Other: _____, on _____
                                                                   Date

_____
Date

Service fee	Miles traveled	Mileage fee	Total fee
$		$	$

_____
Signature

_____
Title

Subscribed and sworn to before me on _____, _____ County, Michigan.
                                           Date

My commission expires: _____ Signature _____ Deputy court clerk/Notary public _____
                  Date

STATE OF MICHIGAN JUDICIAL DISTRICT JUDICIAL CIRCUIT	ORDER FOR SERVICE BY PUBLICATION/POSTING AND NOTICE OF ACTION	CASE NO.

Court address   Court telephone no.

Plaintiff name(s) and address(es)

                               v

Defendant name(s) and address(es)

Plaintiff's attorney, bar no., address, and telephone no.

TO: _____

IT IS ORDERED:

1. You are being sued by plaintiff in this court to _____
_____ . You must file your answer or take other action
permitted by law in this court at the court address above on or before _____ . If you fail to do
Date
so, a default judgment may be entered against you for the relief demanded in the complaint filed in this case.

2. A copy of this order shall be published once each week in _____
    ☐ three consecutive weeks,   Name of publication
for ☐ _____ , and proof of publication shall be filed in this court.

3. _____ shall post a copy of this order in the courthouse, and
 Name
at _____ and
 Location
at _____
 Location
    ☐ three continuous weeks,
for ☐ _____ , and shall file proof of posting in this court.

4. A copy of this order shall be sent to _____ at the last known address
                     Name   ☐ date of the last publication,
by registered mail, return receipt requested, before the ☐ last week of posting,   and the affidavit of mailing shall be
filed with this court.

_____   _____
Date   Judge   Bar no.

AFFIDAVIT OF PUBLISHING

Name of ☐ publisher ☐ agent of publisher	Attach copy of publication here

Name of newspaper	County where published

This newspaper is a qualified newspaper. The attached copy was published in this newpaper for at least 3 consecutive weeks on these dates:

_____

_____   _____
Date   Affiant signature

Subscribed and sworn to before me on _____ , _____ County, Michigan.
                                        Date

My commission expires: _____ Signature: _____
                              Date   Court clerk/Notary public

AFFIDAVIT OF POSTING

I have posted this order in a conspicuous place in the _____ courthouse and the

following places as ordered by this court: _____

_____

_____

It has been posted for   ☐ 3 continous weeks   ☐ _____ continuous weeks   as ordered by this court.

_____   _____
Date   Affiant signature

Subscribed and sworn to before me on _____ , _____ County, Michigan.
                                        Date

My commission expires: _____ Signature: _____
                              Date   Court clerk/Notary public

AFFIDAVIT OF MAILING

	Attach mailing receipt and return receipt here

As ordered, on _____ I mailed a copy of the attached summons and
              Date

complaint and this order to _____
                            Name

at _____ .
    Address

The mailing receipt and return receipt are attached at right.

_____   _____
Date   Affiant signature

Subscribed and sworn to before me on _____ , _____ County, Michigan.
                                        Date

My commission expires: _____ Signature: _____
                              Date   Court clerk/Notary public

Original - Friend of the Court
1st copy - Plaintiff/Attorney
2nd copy - Defendant/Attorney

STATE OF MICHIGAN JUDICIAL CIRCUIT COUNTY	VERIFIED STATEMENT	CASE NO.

1. Mother's last name First name Middle name	2. Any other names by which mother is or has been known

3. Date of birth	4. Social security number	5. Driver license number and state

6. Mailing address and residence address (if different)

7. Eye color	8. Hair color	9. Height	10. Weight	11. Race	12. Scars, tattoos, etc.

13. Home telephone no.	14. Work telephone no.	15. Maiden name	16. Occupation

17. Business/Employer's name and address	18. Gross weekly income

19. Has wife applied for or does she receive public assistance? If yes, please specify kind. ☐ Yes ☐ No	20. AFDC and recipient identification numbers

21. Father's last name First name Middle name	22. Any other names by which father is or has been known

23. Date of birth	24. Social security number	25. Driver license number and state

26. Mailing address and residence address (if different)

27. Eye color	28. Hair color	29. Height	30. Weight	31. Race	32. Scars, tattoos, etc.

33. Home telephone no.	34. Work telephone no.	35. Occupation

36. Business/Employer's name and address	37. Gross weekly income

38. Has husband applied for or does he receive public assistance? If yes, please specify kind. ☐ Yes ☐ No	39. AFDC and recipient identification numbers

40. a. Name of Minor Child Involved in Case	b. Birth Date	c. Age	d. Soc. Sec. No.	e. Residential Address

41. a. Name of Other Minor Child of Either Party	b. Birth Date	c. Age	d. Soc. Sec. No.	e. Residential Address

42. Health care coverage available for each minor child

a. Name of Minor Child	b. Name of Policy Holder	c. Name of Insurance Co./HMO	d. Policy/Certificate/Contract No.

43. Names and addresses of person(s) other than parties, if any, who may have custody of child(ren) during pendency of this case

• If any of the public assistance information above changes before your judgment is entered, you are required to give the Friend of the Court written notice of the change.

I declare that the statements above are true to the best of my information, knowledge, and belief.

Date _____

Signature _____

FOC 23 (5/93) VERIFIED STATEMENT

MCR 3.206(B)

STATE OF MICHIGAN JUDICIAL CIRCUIT COUNTY	ADVICE OF RIGHTS REGARDING USE OF FRIEND OF THE COURT SERVICES	CASE NO.

Friend of the Court address   **Telephone no.**

1. **Right to Refuse Friend of the Court Services**

   a. You have the right to refuse friend of the court services for custody, parenting time, and support. To prevent friend of the court involvement, you must file with the court, along with your first pleading, a motion requesting that friend of the court services not be required. You must attach a signed copy of this advice of rights to the motion. The court will grant the motion provided both parties agree and have signed this advice of rights and it determines that the following are true:

      1) Neither of you receives public assistance for the child(ren) or requests friend of the court services.
      2) There is no evidence of domestic violence or uneven bargaining position between you.
      3) The court finds that declining to receive friend of the court services is not against the best interests of a child.

   b. If you already have a friend of the court case, you can file a motion to discontinue friend of the court services provided both parties agree, and have signed this advice of rights and the court finds that the following are true:

      1) Neither of you receives public assistance for the child(ren) or requests friend of the court services.
      2) There is no evidence of domestic violence or uneven bargaining position between you.
      3) The court finds that declining to receive friend of the court services is not against the best interests of a child.
      4) No money is due the state because of past public assistance.
      5) No arrearage or a custody or parenting time order violation has occurred in the last 12 months.
      6) Neither of you has reopened a friend of the court case in the last 12 months.

2. **Friend of the Court Services (you will not receive these services if you choose not to use the Friend of the Court)**

   The friend of the court must provide the following services for friend of the court cases. You are entitled to these services unless you choose to refuse the services and the court grants that choice.

   a. **Accounting Services**

      Friends of the court must collect support and disburse it within 48 hours. Friend of the court accounting services include: 1) friend of the court accounting for payments received and sent; 2) adjustments of support for parenting time or other credits; and 3) annual statements of accounts, if requested.

   b. **Support Enforcement Services**

      The friend of the court must begin to enforce support when one month of support is overdue. For friend of the court cases, child support enforcement services include:

      • Paying support out of tax refunds.
      • Asking the court to order the nonpaying party to come to court to explain the failure to pay.
      • Having unpaid support paid out of property the payer owns.
      • Reporting support arrearage to a consumer reporting agency or requesting that the payer's licenses be suspended.
      • Collecting support by an income withholding order.

      If you choose not to receive friend of the court services, any existing income withholding source will be notified that the friend of the court is no longer responsible for income withholding. **The parties will be solely responsible for stopping or changing income withholding as the law allows.** The friend of the court will stop any unfinished collection actions.

   c. **Medical Support Enforcement Services**

      The friend of the court is required to recommend how the parents divide health care expenses and to take action to collect the amounts that a parent fails or refuses to pay. When a parent is required to insure the children the friend of the court is authorized to instruct an employer to enroll the children in an insurance plan when the parent fails or refuses to do so.

   d. **Support Review and Modification Services**

      Once every two years persons with friend of the court cases may request the friend of the court to review the support amount. After completing the review, the friend of the court must file a motion to raise or lower support, or inform the parties that it recommends no change. It must also review support when changed circumstances lead it to believe that support should be modified.

Advice of Rights Regarding Use of Friend of the Court Services, continued from page 1

e. Custody and Parenting Time Enforcement Services

For friend of the court cases, the friend of the court must enforce custody and parenting time when a party complains that it is violated. Child custody and parenting time enforcement services include:

- Asking the court to order the noncooperating party to come to the court to explain the failure to obey the parenting time order.
- Suspending the licenses of individuals who deny parenting time.
- Awarding makeup parenting time.
- Joint meetings to resolve complaints.

f. Custody and Parenting Time Investigation Services

For disputes about custody or parenting time in friend of the court cases, the friend of the court sometimes must investigate and provide reports to the parties and the court.

g. Mediation Services

Friend of the court offices must provide mediation services to help parties with friend of the court cases settle custody and parenting time disputes.

3. State Disbursement Unit and IV-D Services

a. State Disbursement Unit (SDU)

If you choose not to receive friend of the court services, you may continue to make payments to, and receive payments through, the state disbursement unit (SDU). The SDU will keep track of the amount paid and sent out. However, the SDU cannot provide you with all of the accounting functions the friend of the court provides.

All payments made through the SDU must be distributed to the amounts due as required by federal law. When a payer has more than one case, federal law determines how a payment is divided among the cases. Even if you choose not to receive friend of the court services, payments through the SDU must be divided among all a payer's cases and distributed in the same manner as payments on FOC cases. You cannot discontinue friend of the court services if you want to use the SDU unless you first provide to the SDU all the information that the SDU needs to set up an account.

b. Your Rights Under Title IV-D of the Social Security Act

Title IV-D of the Social Security Act provides federal government resources to collect child support and it allows certain funding to be used for parenting time and custody services. In Michigan, critical title IV-D services are delivered by the friend of the court. **If you choose not to receive friend of the court services, you cannot receive most IV-D services.**

ACKNOWLEDGMENT REGARDING SERVICES

Check below only if you do not want to receive friend of the court services. Then date and sign. A copy of this document must be attached to your first pleading with the court.

I have read this advice of rights and I understand the friend of the court services I am entitled to receive.

☐ I acknowledge that by signing below **I am choosing not to receive** any friend of the court services. I understand that before this choice can take effect, a motion requesting this choice and the other party's agreement must be filed with the court for approval. I also understand that the court may deny this choice if certain conditions are not met as stated in this advice of rights.

_____	_____	_____	_____
Signature	Date	Signature	Date

If you did not check the above, you are choosing to receive friend of the court services. **For the most effective friend of the court services,** you can request IV-D services by dating and signing below.

I request IV-D services through the friend of the court office.

_____	_____	_____
Date	Signature	Social security number

STATE OF MICHIGAN JUDICIAL CIRCUIT COUNTY	SUPPLEMENTAL NOTICE TO ADVICE OF RIGHTS REGARDING USE OF FRIEND OF THE COURT SERVICES	CASE NO.

Friend of the Court address   **Telephone no.**

1. State Disbursement Unit Payments

a. State Disbursement Unit (SDU)

If you opt out of the friend of the court, you may continue to make payments through the State Disbursement Unit (SDU). The SDU uses the friend of the court for most accounting functions and cannot provide you with all of the accounting functions the friend of the court provides.

For friend of the court cases, payments are made through the SDU and distributed to the amounts due as required by federal law. When a payer has more than one case, federal law determines how a payment is divided between the cases. **Even if parties opt out of the friend of the court, payments through the SDU must be divided between all payer's cases and distributed in the same manner as payments on friend of the court cases.**

b. SDU Limitations

The SDU relies on the friend of the court records to determine the amount of income withholding. The SDU also requires the friend of the court to set up any income withholding or change in income withholding. If you choose not to accept friend of the court services, the SDU will not be able to process payments through income withholding if the person paying support changes jobs or the amount withheld changes.

Under federal law, the state of Michigan is converting its friend of the court to a new single child support enforcement computer system. County friend of the court offices will be converted under a schedule that begins in March, 2003 and continues until September 30, 2003. Until the conversion is completed, only the friend of the court can process checks. If you choose not to accept friend of the court services, you will not be able to use the SDU until all of your cases are converted to MiCSES version 2.4 or greater.

2. Your Acknowledgment of System Limitations on Your Right to Opt Out of Friend of the Court Services

Please sign and return this form to the friend of the court.

I have read this form and I want to opt out of the friend of the court. I understand that I cannot opt out of the friend of the court with SDU services until this case is converted to MiCSES version 2.4 or greater.

_____
Date

_____
Signature

STATE OF MICHIGAN JUDICIAL CIRCUIT COUNTY	ORDER EXEMPTING CASE FROM FRIEND OF THE COURT SERVICES	CASE NO.

Friend of the Court address   FAX no.   Telephone no.

Plaintiff's name and address		Defendant's name and address
	v	

Attorney: Attorney:

Date of hearing: _____   Judge: _____

Bar no.

THE COURT FINDS:

1. There is no evidence of domestic violence or unequal bargaining position between the parties to the case.
2. Granting the parties the relief they have requested would not be against the best interests of any child in the case.
3. The parties have filed executed copies of a form advising them of the services they will not receive if their motion is granted.
4. Neither party receives public assistance for a child in the case.
5. No money is due the state because of past public assistance for a child in the case.
6. No arrearage or custody or parenting time order violation has occurred in the last 12 months in this case.
7. Neither party has reopened a friend of the court case in the last 12 months.
☐ 8. The parties do not want IV-D services and have requested that any existing IV-D case be closed. (Note: This box should be checked unless exceptional circumstances exist that entitle the IV-D case to remain open.)

IT IS ORDERED:

9. Subject to the provisions of item 14 below, this case is not a friend of the court case.
☐ 10. This case is not a title IV-D case. (Note: This box should be checked if item 8 has been checked.)
11. The friend of the court shall not be involved in the enforcement, investigation, or accounting functions for custody, parenting time, or support in this case.
12. The parties are responsible for all enforcement and accounting functions for custody, parenting time, or support in this case.
13. Except as indicated below, there is no income withholding in this case, support will be paid directly by the payer to the payee, and the friend of the court shall terminate any existing income withholding. Should this case become a friend of the court case, the payer must keep the friend of the court advised of the name and address of the payer's source of income and any health care coverage that is available to the payer as a benefit of employment or that the payer maintains including the name of the insurance company, health care organization, or health maintenance organization; the policy, certificate, or contract number; and the names and birth dates of the persons for whose benefit the payer maintains the coverage.
   ☐ a. Support shall be paid through the State Disbursement Unit (SDU). Support shall be paid by income withholding to the extent allowed by statutes and court rules, however, the friend of the court is not responsible for the income withholding. The friend of the court shall notify the employer that it is no longer involved in the case and that any further information concerning income withholding will be provided by the parties.
   ☐ b. Support shall be paid through the SDU.
   If support payments are to be made through the SDU by income withholding or otherwise, the friend of the court shall not close the friend of the court case until the SDU notifies the friend of the court that it has been provided with the information necessary to process the child support payments. There will be no accounting for support that is not paid through the SDU.
14. The friend of the court shall open a friend of the court case if a party applies for public assistance relating to a child of the parties or either party submits to the friend of the court a written request to reopen the friend of the court case. If this case becomes a friend of the court case for any reason, the provisions on the other side of this order shall apply.

_____
Date

_____
Judge

See provisions on back.

CERTIFICATE OF MAILING

I certify that on this date I mailed a copy of this order to the other party by ordinary mail addressed to the last known address.

_____
Date

_____
Signature

FOC 102 (6/03) ORDER EXEMPTING CASE FROM FRIEND OF THE COURT SERVICES   MCL 552.505, MCL 552.505a

If this case becomes a friend of the court case for any reason, the following provisions apply:

1. The parties must cooperate fully with the friend of the court in establishing the case as a friend of the court case.
2. The parties must provide copies of all orders in their case to the friend of the court.
3. The parties must supply any documents that a party to a friend of the court case is required to supply if they have not already done so.
4. The friend of the court is not responsible for determining any support arrearage that is not indicated by payment made through the SDU.
5. Support is payable through the friend of the court effective the date the case becomes a friend of the court case.
6. The friend of the court may prepare and submit, exparte, a uniform child support order that contains all the statutory requirements of a Michigan support order as long as the order does not contradict the existing support order.

| Original - Court | 2nd copy - Plaintiff |
| 1st copy - Friend of the Court | 3rd copy - Defendant |

STATE OF MICHIGAN	REQUEST TO REOPEN	CASE NO.
JUDICIAL CIRCUIT	FRIEND OF THE COURT CASE	
COUNTY		

Friend of the Court address   **Telephone no.**

| Plaintiff's name and address | Defendant's name and address |

Attorney: Attorney:

1. On _____ an order was entered exempting this case from friend of the court services.
   Date

I REQUEST that the friend of the court case be reopened upon filing of this request with the friend of the court office.

CERTIFICATE OF MAILING

I certify that on this date I mailed a copy of this request to the other party by ordinary mail addressed to the last known address.

_____   _____
Date   Signature

FOC 104 (6/03) **REQUEST TO REOPEN FRIEND OF THE COURT CASE**   MCL 552.505, MCL 552.505a

Approved, SCAO

Original - Court
2nd copy - Friend of the Court
3rd copy - Plaintiff
4th copy - Defendant

STATE OF MICHIGAN JUDICIAL CIRCUIT COUNTY	AGREEMENT SUSPENDING IMMEDIATE INCOME WITHHOLDING	CASE NO.

Friend of the Court address

Court telephone no.

Plaintiff's name and address

v

Defendant's name and address

NOTE: MCL 552.604(3); MSA 25.164(4)(3) requires that all new and modified support orders after December 31, 1990 include a provision for immediate income withholding and that income withholding take effect immediately unless the parties enter into a written agreement that the income withholding order shall not take effect immediately.

We understand that by law an order of income withholding in a support order shall take effect immediately. However, we agree to the following:

1. The order of income withholding shall not take effect immediately.

2. An alternative payment arrangement shall be made as follows:

3. Both the payer and the recipient of support shall keep the friend of the court informed of the following:
   a. the name, address, and telephone number of his/her current source of income;
   b. any health care coverage that is available to him/her as a benefit of employment or that is maintained by him/her; the name of the insurance company, health care organization, or health maintenance organization; the policy, certificate or contract number; and the name(s) and birth date(s) of the person(s) for whose benefit s/he maintains health care coverage under the policy, certificate, or contract; and
   c. his/her current residence and mailing address.

4. We further understand that proceedings to implement income withholding shall commence if the payer of support falls one month behind in his/her support payments.

5. We recognize that the court may order withholding of income to take effect immediately for cause or at the request of the payer.

_____
Date

_____
Date

_____
Plaintiff's signature

_____
Defendant's signature

FOC 63 (4/01) **AGREEMENT SUSPENDING IMMEDIATE INCOME WITHHOLDING**

MCL 552.604; MSA 25.164(4)

Approved, SCAO

STATE OF MICHIGAN JUDICIAL CIRCUIT COUNTY	ORDER SUSPENDING IMMEDIATE INCOME WITHHOLDING	CASE NO.

Friend of the Court address   Court telephone no.

Plaintiff's name and address

v

Defendant's name and address

1. Date of hearing: _____ Judge: _____

2. **THE COURT FINDS:**   Bar no.

☐ There is good cause for the order of income withholding not to take effect immediately as follows:

    a. It is in the best interest of the child for immediate income withholding not to take effect for the following stated reasons:

    b. Proof of timely payment of previously ordered support has been provided.

    c. Both the payer and the recipient of support will notify the friend of the court in writing of any change in:

        1) the name, address, and telephone number of his/her current source of income;

        2) any health care coverage that is available to him/her as a benefit of employment or that is maintained by him/her, the name of the insurance company, health care organization, or health maintenance organization; the policy, certificate, or contract number; and the names and birth dates of the persons for whose benefit s/he maintains health care coverage under the policy, certificate, or contract; and

        3) his/her current residence and mailing address within 21 days of the change.

☐ The parties have entered into a written agreement that has been reviewed and entered in the record as follows:

    a. The order of income withholding shall not take effect immediately.

    b. An alternative payment arrangement has been agreed upon (attached).

    c. Both the payer and the recipient of support will notify the friend of the court in writing of any change in:

        1) the name, address, and telephone number of his/her current source of income;

        2) any health care coverage that is available to him/her as a benefit of employment or that is maintained by him/her, the name of the insurance company, health care organization, or health maintenance organization; the policy, certificate, or contract number; and the names and birth dates of the persons for whose benefit s/he maintains health care coverage under the policy, certificate, or contract; and

        3) his/her current residence and mailing address within 21 days of the change.

IT IS ORDERED:

3. Income withholding shall not take effect immediately.

4. Income withholding shall take effect if the fixed amount of arrearage is reached, as specified in law.

_____
Date

_____
Judge

FOC 64 (4/01) **ORDER SUSPENDING IMMEDIATE INCOME WITHHOLDING**

MCL 552.511; MSA 25.176(11),
MCL 552.604; MSA 25.164(4) .

STATE OF MICHIGAN **Circuit Court - Family Division** **COUNTY**	**WAIVER OF MILITARY** **RELIEF LAW RIGHTS**	**CASE NO.**

Plaintiff (appearing *in propria persona*):

Defendant:

v

Defendant says:

1. I am in the active duty of the following unit of the U.S. military:

2. I waive all lawsuit relief rights provided to me in this case by the Soldiers' and Sailors' Civil Relief Act of 1940 and/or Michigan's military relief law (MCL 32.517) or a similar military relief law from another state.

Date _____   Defendant _____

GRP 6 (1/04)   **WAIVER OF MILITARY RELIEF LAW RIGHTS**

Request for Certification of Military Status

TO:

Army Worldwide Locator
U.S. Army Enlisted Records and Evaluation Center
8899 E. 56th St.
Indianapolis, IN 46249-5301
Fee: $3.50 payable by check or money to "Finance Officer"

HQ AFPC/MSIMD
550 C St. West, Suite 50
Randolph AFB, TX 78150-4752
Fee: $3.50 payable by check or money order to "DAO-DE RAFB"

World Wide Locator
Bureau of Naval Personnel
Pers-324D
2 Navy Annex
Washington, DC 20370-3240
Fee: $3.50 payable by check or money to "U.S. Treasurer"

Coast Guard Locator Service
Commanding Officer (RAS)
444 SE Quincy St.
Topeka, KS 66683-3591
Fee: $3.50 payable by check or money order to "U.S. Treasurer"

Headquarters U.S. Marine Corps
Personnel Management Support Branch (MMSB-17)
2008 Elliot Rd.
Quantico, VA 22134-5030
Fee: $3.50 payable by check or money to "U.S. Treasurer"

RE:

Case name _____

Case number _____

Full name of defendant _____

Defendant's date of birth_____

Defendant's social security number _____

Defendant's rank and service number (if known)_____

Defendant's last duty assignment (if known) _____

Defendant's last military address (if known)_____

I am the plaintiff in the above divorce case seeking a default judgment of divorce against the defendant. I must know whether or not the defendant is currently in the active duty of your branch of the U.S. military service, to comply with the Soldiers' and Sailors' Civil Relief Act of 1940 and/or Michigan Compiled Law 32.517 or a similar military relief law from another state.

Please respond with a certificate of the defendant's (non)military status, unit of assignment and military address, if any, as soon as possible. If the defendant is overseas or in a deployed unit, please certify whether the defendant is or is not in active-duty service and omit the other requested information from your response.

A self-addressed stamped envelope is enclosed for your response. A certification fee is also enclosed, but if I qualify for a fee waiver (as spouse), please refund my payment.

Date _____   Signature _____

Name _____

Address _____

_____

Telephone:_____

Military Locator Request

TO:

Army Worldwide Locator
U.S. Army Enlisted Records and Evaluation Center
8899 E. 56th St.
Indianapolis, IN 46249-5301
Fee: $3.50 payable by check or money to "Finance Officer"

HQ AFPC/MSIMD
550 C St. West, Suite 50
Randolph AFB, TX 78150-4752
Fee: $3.50 payable by check or money order to "DAO-DE RAFB"

World Wide Locator
Bureau of Naval Personnel
Pers-324D
2 Navy Annex
Washington, DC 20370-3240
Fee: $3.50 payable by check or money to "U.S. Treasurer"

Coast Guard Locator Service
Commanding Officer (RAS)
444 SE Quincy St.
Topeka, KS 66683-3591
Fee: $3.50 payable by check or money order to "U.S. Treasurer"

Headquarters U.S. Marine Corps
Personnel Management Support Branch (MMSB-17)
2008 Elliot Rd.
Quantico, VA 22134-5030
Fee: $3.50 payable by check or money to "U.S. Treasurer"

RE:

Case name _____

Case number _____

Full name of defendant _____

Defendant's date of birth_____

Defendant's social security number _____

Defendant's rank and service number (if known)_____

Defendant's last duty assignment (if known) _____

Defendant's last military address (if known)_____

    I am the plaintiff in the above case seeking a divorce against the defendant. I request information about the defendant's current rank, service number, unit of assignment and military address. I need this information for service of process, to satisfy the military relief laws and other reasons related to this divorce case.

    A self-addressed stamped envelope is enclosed for your response. A locator fee is also enclosed, but if I qualify for a fee waiver (as spouse), please refund my payment.

Date _____

Signature _____

Name _____

Address _____

_____

Telephone:_____

Original - Court
1st copy - Applicant
Other copies - All appearing parties

STATE OF MICHIGAN	DISMISSAL	CASE NO.
JUDICIAL DISTRICT		
JUDICIAL CIRCUIT		
COUNTY PROBATE		

Court address   Court telephone no.

Plaintiff name(s) and address(es)

v

Defendant name(s) and address(es)

Plaintiff's attorney, bar no., address, and telephone no.

Defendant's attorney, bar no., address, and telephone no.

☐ **NOTICE OF DISMISSAL BY PLAINTIFF**

☐ with
☐ without   prejudice as to:

1. Plaintiff/Attorney for plaintiff files this notice of dismissal of this case
   ☐ all defendants.
   ☐ the following defendant(s): _____

2. I certify, under penalty of contempt, that:
   a. This notice is the first dismissal filed by the plaintiff based upon or including the same claim against the defendant.
   b. All costs of filing and service have been paid.
   c. **No answer or motion has been served upon the plaintiff by the defendant** as of the date of this notice.
   d. A copy of this notice has been provided to the appearing defendant/attorney by ☐ mail ☐ personal service.

_____
Date

_____
Plaintiff/Attorney signature

☐ **STIPULATION TO DISMISS**

☐ with
☐ without   prejudice as to:

I stipulate to the dismissal of this case
☐ all parties.
☐ the following parties: _____

_____
Date

_____
Plaintiff/Attorney signature

_____
Date

_____
Defendant/Attorney signature

☐ **ORDER TO DISMISS**

☐ with
☐ without

IT IS ORDERED this case is dismissed   prejudice. Conditions, if any: _____

_____

_____

_____
Date

_____
Judge

_____
Bar no.

MC 09 (6/97) **DISMISSAL**   MCR 2.504

<table>
<tr><td>STATE OF MICHIGAN
Circuit Court - Family Division
COUNTY</td><td>JUDGMENT OF DIVORCE
Page 2 of   pages</td><td>CASE NO.</td></tr>
</table>

Plaintiff:

Defendant:

v

IT IS ALSO ORDERED:

13. SPOUSAL SUPPORT:

14. PAYMENT OF SUPPORT: Spousal support shall be paid

by ☐ immediate income withholding ☐ without income withholding until past-due support equals or exceeds the monthly amount of support

to ☐ state disbursement unit (SDU). ☐ directly to the payee. ☐ other:

15. PAST-DUE SUPPORT:

a. **Retroactive modification.** Support is an order the date it is due and shall not be modified retroactively except as allowed by MCL 552.603 and 552.603b.

b. **Lien and surcharge.** Unpaid support is a lien on the payer's property by operation of law and the payer's property can be encumbered or seized if past-due support exceeds two times the monthly amount of periodic support payments. In a friend of the court case, a surcharge will be added to past-due support as provided by MCL 552.603a.

16. FRIEND OF THE COURT SERVICES AND FEES:

☐ a. **Friend of the court opt-out.** This case shall be opted out of the following friend of the court services: ☐ all friend of the court services ☐ all friend of the court services except collection and distribution of spousal support through the SDU ☐ immediate income withholding only

b. **Friend of the court fees.** While a friend of the court case, the support payer shall pay friend of the court service fees and other statutory fees.

17. PERSONAL INFORMATION: The parties' current residence addresses and telephone nos. appear in the main caption of this judgment. Their current sources of income are listed below:

	Plaintiff	**Defendant**
Source of income:		
Address:		
Telephone no:		

The parties have previously provided information about their health care coverage, social security nos., driver's and occupational licenses. In a friend of the court case, they must inform the friend of the court of any changes or additions to the personal information cited in this section, reporting changes in their residence information in writing within 21 days of a change.

GRP 4x   (1/04)   **JUDGMENT OF DIVORCE, page 2**

Original - Court
1st copy - Friend of the Court

2nd copy - Plaintiff
3rd copy - Defendant
Additional copies to all sources of income

STATE OF MICHIGAN JUDICIAL CIRCUIT COUNTY	INCOME WITHHOLDING ORDER ☐ Court ordered ☐ Consent	CASE NO.

Friend of the Court address   **Court telephone no.**

Plaintiff's name and address

v

Defendant's name and address

Regarding: _____
                            Payer

_____
Social security number

Date of order: _____

Judge: _____

1. The court finds that the above payer owes current support, statutory fees, and/or arrearages in the above case, and notice has been given as required by law.

2. Income is defined as: commissions, earnings, salaries, wages, and other income due now or in the future from an employer and successor employers; any payment due now or in the future from a profit-sharing plan, pension plan, insurance contract, annuity, unemployment compensation, supplemental unemployment benefits, and worker's compensation; any amount of money due the payer under a support order as a debt of any other individual, partnership, association, private or public corporation, the United States or any Federal agency, any state or political subdivision of any state, or any other legal entity indebted to the payer.

IT IS ORDERED:

3. The source of income shall withhold payer's income as specified in the attached notice of income withholding and in any subsequent notices.

4. The State Disbursement Unit shall receive and disburse these funds for the purpose of collecting support, statutory fees, and the payment of all arrearages.

5. Any income withheld under this order shall be paid to the State Disbursement Unit within 3 days after the date of withholding.

6. If the payer's existing support order is modified by an order of the court, the office of the friend of the court shall send a notice of modification to the source of income by ordinary mail. The amount assigned or withheld shall be changed to conform with the court modification within 7 days after receipt of the notice of modification.

_____   _____   _____
Signature of preparer   Judge   Bar no.

☐ I consent to the terms of this order.
_____
Payer's signature

CERTIFICATE OF MAILING

I certify that on this date I mailed a copy of this order to the parties and sources of income by ordinary mail addressed to their last known addresses.

_____   _____
Date   Signature

FOC 5 (4/01) **INCOME WITHHOLDING ORDER**   MCL 552.601 et seq.; MSA 25.164(1) et ʳ

STATE OF MICHIGAN THIRD JUDICIAL CIRCUIT WAYNE COUNTY	CERTIFICATE OF CONFORMITY FOR DOMESTIC RELATIONS ORDER OR JUDGMENT	CASE NO.

Penobscot Bldg. 645 Griswold Ave. Detroit, MI 48226   313-224-5372

PLAINTIFF'S NAME		DEFENDANT'S NAME

V.

I certify the attached Order or Judgment as presented for entry to be in full conformity with the requirements set forth by statute, **INCLUDING A PROVISION FOR IMMEDIATE INCOME WITHHOLDING (WHICH SHALL BE IMPLEMENTED BY THE FRIEND OF THE COURT), THE PAYER'S SOCIAL SECURITY NUMBER AND THE NAME AND ADDRESS OF HIS/HER SOURCE OF INCOME IF KNOWN , UNLESS OTHERWISE ORDERED BY THE COURT,** and with Michigan Court Rules 3.201 and following, and if applicable, includes all provisions of the Friend of the Court recommendation or is in conformity with the decision of

_____ rendered on the _____ day of

_____ , 19 _____ .

_____
Date

_____
Attorney / Bar No.

Instructions :   Please sign and present this Certificate to the Court Clerk when the Order or Judgment is presented for entry. If an ex parte interim order is being presented to the Judge, please complete the "Certificate on Behalf of Plaintiff regarding Ex Parte Interim Support Order" and follow Local Court Rule 3.206.

#1225 (7/95) CERTIFICATE OF CONFORMITY FOR DOMESTIC RELATIONS ORDER OR JUDGMENT

DISCOVERY
101

www.discovery101.com

A Special Thanks to Author, Jen Karofsky

For more information, please contact:

Discovery 101, Inc.
85 Partridge Lane
Concord, MA 01742

CPSIA Code: PRT0911A
ISBN: 1-936319-88-8
ISBN-13: 978-1-936319-88-6

Printed in the United States

Travis and Taylor
Discover
SOCCER

written by
Jay Heaps & Discovery 101
Illustrated by Danny Moore

Welcome!

Hey Discoverers! We're Travis and Taylor, The Discovery Twins! Welcome to Soccer 101, where we invite you to join us on a journey of fun, adventure, learning and discovery...all about the great game of Soccer. In this book, **Travis and Taylor Discover Soccer**, you can read along and learn all about soccer. We also invite you to use the other activities and games in your Soccer 101 Discovery Pack to further your soccer discovery, such as the Discovery Cards, Memory Cards, Video and Soccer Discovery Book. Remember, you can also use your computer to play all the games and activities in your Discovery Pack. Just ask your parents or teacher to help you. Happy Discovering!

"Travis! Taylor! The mail's here...and it looks there is a package for each of you!"

"How cool!" Taylor shouted.

"Do you think it's a new Discovery Pack? I wonder who it's from?" Travis said to Taylor.

"Look there's a note!" said Taylor.

Travis and Taylor ran back to the kitchen table to open the special note just for them. The note read:

Dear Travis and Taylor,

I hope you guys are doing well! I really need your help... and fast! I am coaching my soccer team in Saturday's tournament and we need two more players. I need you to spend the week learning about Soccer. I am giving you these Soccer Discovery Packs so you can learn more about the game and how to play it. I'd also like you to join me at practice today. I am looking forward to a fun week. See you on the field shortly.

Love,

Uncle Adam

Travis and Taylor immediately opened their Soccer Discovery Packs and examined all the fun things inside.

After breakfast, Travis and Taylor ran up to their rooms and put on their soccer **uniforms**.

"I'm wearing my green jersey!" said Travis. "I'm wearing my pink shorts!" said Taylor.

uniform

Soccer 101

Travis and Taylor soon arrived on the field where Uncle Adam was there to greet them. "Glad you could make it kids, you're just in time to practice with the team. Hurry up and put on your shin guards and cleats!"

shin guards Soccer 101

cleats Soccer 101

"Alright team! Grab your **soccer balls** and let's get started. Practice has begun!" shouted Uncle Adam.

soccer ball

Soccer
1 0 1

Uncle Adam started the practice with a lap around the soccer field. "Hey Taylor, I remember from our Discovery Cards that the **field** is in the shape of a rectangle," said Travis. "Lets join them for the run! It's great practice and great exercise!"

Next, Uncle Adam asked the team to form two groups, and the team began practicing dribbling skills.

"Cool!" said Taylor excitedly. "We get to dribble the soccer ball now. It looks tricky!"

dribble

"You guys are doing a great job controlling the soccer ball," said Uncle Adam, "but now let's take a quick break and talk about the game." After the team sat down to rest, Uncle Adam asked, "What are we trying to do in soccer, guys?"

"Score a goal!" yelled the team. "Correct!" said Uncle Adam.

goal

Soccer 101

Uncle Adam continued to explain the rules of soccer. "There are many positions on a soccer team. Travis and Taylor, can you take out your Discovery Cards and share them with the team?"

Travis took out the **offense** Discovery Card to show the team. "Offense is the team who has the ball and is trying to score a goal."

Next, Taylor jumped up and pulled out the defense Discovery Card. "The team trying to stop the offense from scoring a goal is the defense."

"Great job!" said Uncle Adam. "You guys are really starting to understand the game of soccer."

defense

"Also," said Travis, "Each team has a goalie."

"I know what the goalies do," Taylor chimed in. "They stop the other team from scoring."

"Yes!" Uncle Adam added, "and goalies are the only players on the field that are allowed to use their hands."

goalie

Soccer
101

"Okay, kids, please grab your soccer balls and let's continue practicing," said Uncle Adam. "We are now going to work on how to **pass** the ball."

"What is a pass?" asked Taylor. "It's when you use your feet to move the ball to someone else on your team," answered Travis. He then passed the ball across the field to Taylor. "Cool! Nice pass!" yelled Taylor.

pass

Soccer
1&1

Next, Uncle Adam had them line up in front of the goal for the last activity of the day. "Pretend that I'm a goalie," he said. "Try to **kick** the ball past me and into the goal."

Travis looked excitedly at Taylor, "Awesome!" he said.

After practice was over, Travis and Taylor grabbed their Discovery Packs and waved goodbye to their new teammates.

"Don't forget to practice all the new skills you learned today," said Uncle Adam. "You will need them for the big game this Saturday!"

kick

Soccer 101

Travis and Taylor spent the rest of the week discovering soccer. Saturday soon arrived and Travis and Taylor were super excited. They ran onto the field in their uniforms to meet Uncle Adam and the team. The Twins waved to their mom and dad who were sitting in seats near the sideline to watch the game.

sideline

Soccer 101

"Are you ready for the big game, team?" asked Uncle Adam with a big smile on his face.

"We practiced and practiced all week long," said Taylor.

"You bet we are!" said the team.

The **referee** walked out onto the field. When he blew his whistle, the team knew the game was about to start. Uncle Adam turned to his team, "You all have worked so hard this week, and I'm really proud of each and every one of you. Now go out there, do your best, and have fun!"

referee

Soccer
101

coin toss

"Let's start the game with the **coin toss**," the referee announced. "The winner will decide who plays offense and who plays defense first." Uncle Adam took Travis to the middle of the field to meet a player from the other team.

While Travis was gone, Taylor took out her Discovery Cards to check what a coin toss really was.

Uncle Adam's team won the coin toss. They decided to start with the ball. The game began. Both teams played hard, and after several minutes each had scored a goal.

The teams took a short break to get some water. "Okay,"
Uncle Adam said. "We have one minute left. You guys have
been playing really well. Let's try and score another goal!"

When they got back on the field, Travis began to dribble the
soccer ball up the field and toward the other team's goal.

"It's my turn now," Taylor shouted. "Pass the ball to me...
   I'm open, and I'm ready to score a goal. That net is mine!"

"Here, Taylor!" Travis passed the ball across the field to his sister.

She then took a deep breath and kicked the ball with
all her might.

GOOOOOOOOOOOOOOOOOOAL!

"We did it...together!" The team jumped up and down.
"It's the power of teamwork!" Both teams lined up to
shake hands with one another. "Great job," Travis said
to the other team. "You guys played really well, too!"
exclaimed Taylor.

Taylor turned to Uncle Adam. "Thank you, Uncle Adam!
We had a great time discovering soccer this week."

After celebrating with their new friends, Travis and Taylor
walked with their mom and dad to the car and waved
goodbye to everyone. Uncle Adam winked back.

The next day, Travis and Taylor decided they wanted to keep practicing their new soccer skills. Before they headed outside, they grabbed a healthy snack in the kitchen and sat down at the computer to email their Uncle Adam.

Dear Uncle Adam,

Thank you so much for sending us our Soccer Discovery Packs. We thought we knew so much about soccer already, but now we know...there's always more to discover! We loved learning about all the positions on the soccer field and about the rules of the game. But most importantly, we loved making new friends and working together. Thanks for showing us that discovering new things is lots of fun!"

Love,

Travis and Taylor

Okay Discoverers...
Now it's your turn...You're up!

Soccer 101

Glossary

(All 15 Terms can be found on your Soccer 101 Discovery cards!)

Uniform—The matching outfit that all of the players on a soccer team wear.

Shin Guards—Pads worn by soccer players to protect the front of their legs from knee to ankle.

Cleats—Special shoes used in soccer that stop soccer players from sliding.

Soccer Ball—A ball used for playing soccer.

Field—The area where a soccer game is played.

Dribble—When a soccer player kicks the ball in short, soft kicks to move it around the soccer field.

Goal—The net a soccer ball must go into for a goal to be scored.

Offense—The team that has the ball and is trying to score a goal.

Defense—The team that does not have the ball and is protecting their goal.

Goalie—The soccer player who tries to stop the other team from scoring by preventing the ball from going into the goal.

Pass—To kick a ball to another player on your team.

Kick—A quick movement with the foot or feet to move the ball.

Sideline—The long white lines down the two sides of the soccer field.

Referee—The person on the field in the yellow or striped shirt that makes sure the soccer players are following the rules of the game.

Coin Toss—The flipping of a coin in the air to determine which team starts the game with control of the ball.

Find all of your Discovery 101
needs and links at:

www.discovery101.com

Follow us on:

 www.facebook.com/discovery101

 www.twitter.com/D101Tweet

 www.youtube.com/discovery101

DISCOVERY
101